A Beginner's 10-Step Guide to Understanding
the Basics and Growing Your Dream Garden

BACKYARD VEGETABLE GARDENING MADE SIMPLE

LAUREN MOORE

TABLE OF CONTENTS

INTRODUCTION

Welcome to the world of backyard gardening!

Calling all aspiring green thumbs and future garden gurus! Are you a budding gardener staring out at your backyard, wondering how to transform it into a garden oasis? Do you dream of harvesting your own homegrown produce and experiencing the sheer joy of watching plants thrive under your care? If you've ever pondered how to embark on this green journey, well, you've just unearthed the ultimate guide to make your gardening dreams sprout to life!

Gardening isn't just about pretty flowers and tasty vegetables; it's an art, a science, and a deeply satisfying endeavor. There are plenty of joys and benefits when it comes to gardening. Just picture it: You are basking in the glory of lush, green plants that you've lovingly nurtured from tiny seeds. As they grow, so does your sense of accomplishment and the sheer joy of watching nature flourish under your care. It's like having a front-row seat to the world's most captivating show. With each new leaf, blossom, and fruit you become part of a natural masterpiece.

But hold on! There is a lot more to gardening than meets the eye. It's a source of endless wonder, a sanctuary for stress relief, and a bountiful provider of fresh, homegrown produce. Imagine stepping into your garden and plucking a sun-ripened tomato, the taste of which is a revelation compared to store-bought varieties. This is the magic of gardening—a tapestry of colors, flavors, and aromas that you can create right in your own backyard.

Starting and having a backyard garden can bring a wide range of benefits, both for your physical well-being and your overall quality of life. Here are some of the key advantages:

- fresh, healthy produce

  o One of the most obvious benefits is having access to fresh, homegrown fruits, vegetables, and herbs. These are often more nutritious and flavorful than store-bought options.

- cost savings

  o Growing your own produce can lead to significant savings on your grocery bills. The initial investment in seeds and gardening supplies can pay off in the long run.

- physical exercise

  o Gardening is a form of low-impact exercise that can help improve your fitness. Activities like digging, planting, weeding, and harvesting keep you active and engaged.

- stress reduction

  - Spending time in the garden has been shown to reduce stress and promote relaxation. The act of gardening, surrounded by nature, can have a calming effect on the mind.

- improved mental health

  - Gardening can boost your mood and mental well-being. It provides a sense of accomplishment, and the process of nurturing plants can be therapeutic.

- connection to nature

  - Having a garden allows you to connect with the natural world. You can observe the changing seasons, watch wildlife, and create a habitat for pollinators like bees and butterflies.

- enhanced home aesthetics

  - A well-maintained garden can significantly enhance the beauty and curb appeal of your home. It provides a peaceful and inviting outdoor space for relaxation and socializing.

- education and learning

  - Gardening offers continuous learning opportunities. You can acquire knowledge about plant biology, soil science, pest management, and sustainable gardening practices.

- environmental benefits

  - Growing your own food reduces your carbon footprint by decreasing the need for transportation and packaging. Additionally, sustainable gardening practices can improve soil health and reduce water consumption.

- community building

  - Gardens can foster a sense of community. Sharing surplus produce with neighbors or participating in local gardening clubs can help you connect with like-minded individuals.

- self-sufficiency

  - In times of crisis or emergency, a backyard garden can provide a valuable source of fresh food, contributing to greater self-sufficiency.

- teaching and bonding

  - Gardening can be a fantastic activity for families. It offers an opportunity to teach children about nature, responsibility, and where food comes from while spending quality time together.

- creativity and expression

    - Designing and tending to your garden allows for self-expression and creativity. You can experiment with various plants, colors, and layouts to create a unique outdoor space.

A backyard garden is not just about growing plants; it's about nurturing your physical and mental health, connecting with nature, and enjoying the many rewards that come with cultivating your own piece of green paradise. Whether you're a seasoned gardener or a novice, the benefits of having a backyard garden are bountiful and enriching.

Maybe that all sounds too good to be true, but the truth is, it is just a page turn away. This book is your key to unlocking the secrets of successful backyard gardening. I'm here to guide you through every step, from turning your backyard into a thriving garden oasis to enjoying the fruits of your labor.

Throughout the following pages, we'll explore the 10 essential steps to transform your backyard into a green haven. Each chapter is designed to provide you with practical insights, expert tips, and a clear roadmap to success. By the time you've turned the final page, you'll have not only gained the knowledge and skills necessary to be a successful gardener but also the confidence to embark on this rewarding journey.

We're talking about the 10 essential steps that will take your backyard from a barren wasteland to a thriving, green paradise. Whether you're a budding gardener or just looking to hone your horticultural skills, you're in the right place.

So, don your gardening gloves, grab your trusty trowel, and let's get started. Together, we'll cultivate your backyard into a thriving garden, one chapter at a time. Are you ready to dig in and discover the world of backyard gardening? Let's begin.

CHAPTER 1:
Understanding Your Space

The first stop on our journey, my green-thumb enthusiast, on how to turn your outdoor space into a thriving oasis of beauty and abundance is to understand the garden you have. In this chapter, we embark on a journey that will have you navigating sunlight, shade, and soil like a seasoned horticulturist. To create a successful garden, you must first understand the canvas on which you're about to paint your masterpiece—the unique characteristics of your gardening space.

Assessing Your Backyard: Sunlight, Shade, and Soil

Let's explore the importance of sunlight in gardening and how to assess and utilize sunlight effectively in your garden.

Sunlight is a fundamental factor in gardening due to its critical role in plant growth.

Here's why sunlight is so essential:

1. Photosynthesis

Sunlight is the primary source of energy for plants. Through photosynthesis, plants convert sunlight into chemical energy, specifically glucose, which is used as fuel for growth and development.

2. Plant growth

Adequate sunlight is crucial for plant growth. It enables plants to produce the sugars and starches they need for structural growth, flowering, and fruiting. Without sufficient sunlight, plants can become stunted and less productive.

3. Flowering and fruiting

Sunlight is a key trigger for flowering in many plant species. It also influences the size, color, and quality of flowers and fruits. Insufficient sunlight can result in fewer or less vibrant blooms and smaller, less flavorful fruits.

4. Health and vitality

Plants exposed to the right amount of sunlight tend to be healthier and more vigorous. They are better equipped to resist diseases and pests and are more likely to thrive.

When it comes to plants, not all of them have the same sunlight requirements. We can divide them into three categories: those who need full sun, partial shade, and full shade.

Full Sun

Plants that thrive in full sun require at least 6-8 hours of direct sunlight each day. There are many varieties to choose from including plants such as

- tomato
- bell pepper
- sunflower
- zinnia
- marigold
- basil
- rosemary
- lavender
- coreopsis
- salvia

Partial Shade

Partial shade plants can tolerate some sunlight but prefer protection from the intense midday sun. These plants typically thrive with 3-6 hours of sunlight per day and include plants such as

- lettuce
- spinach
- mint
- chives
- cilantro
- bleeding heart

- astilbe
- columbine
- hosta
- fern

Full Shade

Plants that thrive in full shade receive little to no direct sunlight, although some of them might enjoy some filtered sunlight that comes through the trees. Full shade plants include plants such as

- hosta
- fern
- impatiens
- coleus
- coral bells
- lungwort
- bleeding heart
- lamium
- hellebore
- pachysandra

In order to have a successful thriving garden, you need to identify the different sunspots in your garden and how the sun moves throughout the day. To do this, you can use a technique called sun mapping.

Sun mapping offers many advantages as it provides insights into specific sunlight conditions in different garden areas. It also helps us to identify spots with morning sun, intense midday sun, and areas that remain shaded during various times. And it's very easy to do; it only requires a relaxing day in the sun and observation.

Spend a day in your backyard observing sunlight patterns. Take note of which areas receive the most sunlight and which remain shaded during various parts of the day.

Armed with knowledge from your sun map, you can strategically plan your garden layout and plant placement based on sunlight requirements. This ensures that each plant receives the optimal amount of sunlight for its growth and health. This brings us to plant placement and sunlight.

Plant Placement

As we have already discovered, different plants have different sunlight requirements. By strategically placing your plants, you can ensure that they all receive the maximum amount of light they need.

Let's take tall versus short plants as an example. You want to position tall plants, such as sunflowers or trellised vegetables like tomatoes, so they won't block sunlight from reaching shorter plants. This ensures that all plants receive their fair share of sunlight, promoting uniform growth and healthy development.

By understanding the role of sunlight in plant growth, identifying sunlight preferences among different plant species, and creating a sun map of your garden, you can strategically plan your garden layout and plant placement to optimize sunlight exposure. This foundational knowledge is key to a successful and visually appealing garden, ensuring that your plants thrive and produce abundantly.

Soil: Laying a Foundation

Soil is the very foundation of gardening success. It provides physical support for plant roots and serves as a reservoir for crucial nutrients and water. Healthy soil is teeming with life, hosting beneficial microorganisms, earthworms, and other organisms that contribute to nutrient cycling and plant health. The soil's composition, texture, and fertility directly impact the growth, vigor, and productivity of your plants.

If you want to know whether or not your garden soil is of good quality, here are characteristics of good soil you can watch out for:

- Good soil should have a crumbly texture that is easy to work with and allows for proper root penetration.

- It consists of a balanced mix of sand, silt, and clay, with their proportions varying based on plant requirements. Loam soil, which combines all three in ideal proportions, is often considered the best for most plants.

- Soil pH is another crucial factor. Most plants thrive in soils with a slightly acidic to neutral pH (around 6 to 7). However, some plants have specific pH preferences, so it's essential to match the soil pH to the plants you intend to grow.

Earthworms are very good indicators when it comes to soil health:

- Earthworms are indicators of soil quality and health. Their presence signifies fertile, well-aerated soil rich in organic matter.

- Earthworms play a vital role in improving soil structure through their burrowing activities, creating channels for air and water movement.

- They break down organic materials like decaying leaves, enriching the soil with nutrients. The castings (worm excrement) left behind by earthworms are nutrient-rich and enhance soil fertility.

So, if you want to know if you have healthy soil, check for earthworms. If there are none or only a few small ones, you may need to amend your soil and work out a watering schedule.

Amending soil involves improving its structure, fertility, and nutrient content. Organic matter is a key component in this process. Adding organic matter, such as compost, well-rotted manure, or peat moss, enhances soil structure by increasing pore space and improving aeration. Organic matter also provides a slow-release source of essential nutrients, enhancing the soil's fertility and promoting plant health. Furthermore, organic matter fosters the development of beneficial microorganisms that aid in nutrient cycling.

Just like you observe your garden and do sun mapping, observe your garden soil and make sure that it drains well.

Proper soil drainage is essential for preventing waterlogged roots. When soil is waterlogged, it lacks the necessary oxygen levels for root respiration, leading to root rot and plant stress. Well-draining soil allows excess water to move away from the root zone, maintaining a balance of air and water in the soil.

The ideal soil for most plants contains a balanced mix of sand, silt, and clay. Sand provides good drainage, silt offers fertility, and clay retains moisture. The right proportions vary depending on the specific plant's needs.

The percolation test is a simple method to assess your soil's drainage capabilities. To perform the test, dig a hole in your garden. Fill the hole with water and observe how long it takes for the water to drain. Well-draining soil should clear out excess water within a day. If the water remains for longer, it indicates poor drainage, and you may need to take steps to improve the soil's drainage characteristics.

In summary, nurturing healthy and well-draining soil is fundamental for gardening success. Proper soil assessment, drainage improvement, and organic matter incorporation contribute to an environment where plants can thrive. Soil is the canvas upon which your garden grows, and its care and preparation are essential for bountiful harvests and vibrant plants. Don't worry, we'll dig deeper into the soil a little later on.

Choosing the Right Spot for Your Garden

It may sound weird that you have to choose the right spot for your garden; your garden can't move—it's your backyard and you can't exactly just move it. That is all very true but what I mean by choosing the right spot for your garden is you need to keep certain things in mind when planning your garden. For example, if you plant your veggies in the farthest corner of your garden out of sight, the chances are you might neglect them. Rather, plant your edibles closer to your home and your aesthetic plants further away.

Choosing the right spot for your garden involves several strategic considerations that can greatly impact your gardening experience and the success of your plants.

Let's have a closer look at each aspect.

1. Convenient Location: Your Garden's Accessibility

The first aspect when it comes to planning your garden is accessibility. When it comes to gardening, you want everything you are going to use and your garden to be as close as possible. Placing your edible garden close to your home has several advantages:

- better monitoring
  - Being nearby allows you to keep a close eye on your plants. This proximity makes it easier to spot any signs of trouble, such as pests, diseases, or dry soil, promptly. Early detection of issues enables you to take immediate

action to mitigate problems and prevent them from spreading.

- stronger connection with plants
  - Frequent visits to your garden fosters a stronger connection with your plants. When you're regularly in close proximity to your garden, you become more attuned to its needs. This emotional connection often results in better care and attention, ultimately benefiting your plants' health and growth.

- optimal harvest timing
  - Proximity to your garden ensures that you're more likely to harvest your crops at their peak ripeness. You won't miss the optimal harvest window, which can be critical for certain crops like fruits and vegetables. Harvesting at the right time enhances the flavor and quality of your produce.

Naturally, garden accessibility encompasses not only your vegetables and herbs but also extends to all your other plants. Plan your garden layout to ensure that you can easily monitor all your plants and move freely throughout the entire garden space.

2. Ease of Maintenance

The second aspect when it comes to your garden layout is making maintenance easy for yourself. A garden that is conveniently located near essential resources not only saves time and energy but offers various other benefits as well:

- time and energy savings
    - When your garden is situated close to your hose, compost pile, gardening tools, and storage, you save significant time and energy. You won't need to make lengthy trips back and forth, which can be physically taxing, especially during busy gardening seasons.

- efficient gardening
    - Proximity to resources means that you can quickly access what you need, promoting efficient gardening practices. For example, if you notice a pest infestation or a wilting plant, you can grab the necessary tools or supplies promptly to address the issue.

- enhanced organization
    - A garden with nearby resources encourages better organization. You can maintain a neat and orderly garden shed or storage area for your gardening equipment, making it easier to find what you need when you need it.

Having all the resources you need close by really makes regular maintenance a breeze. Ease of maintenance not only simplifies gardening but also promotes regular garden care, such as

- weeding
    - With resources at your fingertips, you're more likely to tackle tasks like weeding regularly. This proactive approach prevents weeds from taking over and competing with your plants for resources.

- watering
    - Prompt access to a nearby water source, like a hose, encourages consistent and adequate watering. Proper hydration is essential for plant health, and having water nearby ensures you can water your garden when it's needed most, especially during dry spells.

- pruning and trimming
    - Regular pruning and trimming are essential for shaping plants, removing dead or diseased branches, and encouraging healthy growth. When your tools are within reach, you're more likely to perform these tasks as needed, contributing to the overall well-being of your garden.

- timely pest control
    - If you detect pests or diseases, quick action is vital. Being close to your gardening tools allows you to address these issues promptly, minimizing potential damage to your plants.

Designing your garden for ease of maintenance by considering the proximity of essential resources can significantly impact your gardening experience. It saves you time and energy, fosters efficient gardening practices, and encourages regular maintenance, all of which contribute to a healthier and more productive garden.

3. Water Accessibility

As briefly mentioned, having a water source close to your garden makes gardening easier. However, not only is having a water source nearby or bringing a water source close to your garden convenient for you but having an adequate water supply is crucial for your garden's health.

- consistent soil moisture
    - Proximity to a water source ensures that you can maintain consistent soil moisture levels. This is particularly important during dry periods or when you're growing thirsty crops. Plants rely on a steady supply of water to absorb nutrients and stay hydrated. Convenient access to water allows you to meet these needs without delays.

- efficient watering methods
    - Having a water source nearby allows you to implement efficient watering methods like drip irrigation. Drip irrigation delivers water directly to the roots of plants, reducing water wastage through evaporation or runoff.

It also saves you time and resources by targeting water where it's needed most.

4. Expansion Possibility

As you map out your garden, always leave room for change and expansion. As you grow along with your plants and become a better gardener, you may want to make your garden bigger, add new features, or change things up.

- proactive planning
  - Planning for potential expansion from the beginning is a wise strategy. Consider areas within your garden layout where you might want to add more beds or plant additional crops or other plants. This proactive approach eliminates the need for a complete garden overhaul later on, saving you time and effort.

- aesthetic cohesion
  - Designing your garden with expansion in mind ensures that it remains aesthetically cohesive as it grows. Your garden will maintain its overall design integrity, and new additions will seamlessly blend with the existing layout. This creates an appealing and harmonious visual experience.

In summary, these considerations emphasize the advantages of placing your garden in proximity to your home, ensuring ease of maintenance, providing access to water, and planning for future growth. These strategic decisions contribute to a healthier, more enjoyable gardening experience while maximizing the potential of your garden space.

Protection Against Wildlife and Pests

Sometimes when we are planning our gardens, we get so excited and occupied with what and where to plant that we often forget to make provisions for protection against threats that we have not seen yet. Including protective measures in your garden plan is essential to protect your garden from wildlife and pests.

Fencing

Fencing is a highly effective method to protect your garden from various types of wildlife and pests. Here are some key things to keep in mind should you need to erect a fence or wildlife-proof your current one:

1. Larger animal deterrence

    A. Fencing acts as a physical barrier that can deter larger animals like deer, rabbits, groundhogs, and even neighborhood pets from entering your garden. These animals can cause significant damage by nibbling on plants or digging in the soil.

2. Material selection

    A. When choosing fencing materials, consider both functionality and aesthetics. You want the fence to serve its purpose while also complementing the overall look of your garden.

B. Common materials include wood, vinyl, metal, or even mesh. The choice often depends on your garden's style and your budget.

3. Height and depth

A. The height of your fence is crucial, especially for animals that can jump or climb. Ensure that the fence is tall enough to deter these animals.

B. Additionally, some pests, like rodents, may burrow under fences, so it's wise to extend the fence below ground level to prevent them from digging their way in.

While fences can help keep out wildlife and neighborhood dogs who want to look for buried bones in your garden, unfortunately, fences can't keep out the smaller pests.

Natural Deterrents (Companion Planting)

The best natural pest management method is companion planting. We'll go into more detail a little later on, but for now, all you need to know is that companion planting involves strategically planting certain flowers or herbs alongside your crops to deter pests and promote a healthier garden ecosystem.

Let's briefly look at how it works:

- pest repelling plants
  - Companion planting relies on the natural pest-repelling properties of specific plants. For instance, marigolds are known for deterring aphids, nematodes, and other insect pests. Basil is effective at repelling flies and mosquitoes. By interspersing these plants among your crops, you create a protective barrier that pests find less appealing.

- beauty and diversity
  - One of the advantages of companion planting is that it not only safeguards your plants but also adds visual appeal and diversity to your garden. These pest-repelling plants can contribute different colors, textures, and fragrances to your garden, enhancing its overall aesthetics.

- beneficial insects
  - Companion planting doesn't stop at pest deterrence; it also attracts beneficial insects. Some plants, like yarrow and dill, attract ladybugs, lacewings, and parasitic wasps—natural predators of many garden pests. Encouraging these beneficial insects to visit your garden helps maintain a balanced ecosystem and reduces the need for chemical pesticides.

Using fencing and companion planting as methods for protecting your garden from wildlife and pests is a smart and eco-friendly approach. Fencing provides a physical barrier against larger animals, while companion planting leverages the natural repellent properties of certain plants and fosters a diverse and beneficial garden environment. Combining these methods can help you maintain a thriving and pest-free garden.

Good Airflow

Airflow is a term that you definitely will encounter sooner or later on your gardening journey—let's make it sooner. While you map out your garden and decide on what to plant and where to plant it, keep in mind that there needs to be enough space between plants so there will be enough airflow around them. Apart from plant spacing, regular running plants that can be pruned also help with airflow.

Plant Spacing

Proper plant spacing is crucial for maintaining good airflow in your garden:

- preventing overcrowding
  - Overcrowded plants can lead to reduced air circulation, which in turn creates a favorable environment for moisture-related issues like mildew and fungal diseases. Plants need space to breathe and access sunlight and fresh air.

- disease prevention
  - ○ Adequate spacing allows air to move freely between plants, which helps to reduce humidity and moisture buildup. This, in turn, lowers the risk of fungal diseases. Plants that are too close together can trap moisture and create a microenvironment conducive to disease development.

- uniform growth
  - ○ Proper spacing promotes uniform growth among your plants. When plants are evenly spaced, they can develop without competition for resources like sunlight, water, and nutrients. This leads to healthier and more robust plants.

- spacing guidelines
  - ○ Plant spacing varies depending on the specific crop and its mature size. Refer to seed packets or plant labels for recommended spacing guidelines. For example, larger plants like tomatoes may require 18-24 inches between each plant, while smaller crops like lettuce can be spaced more closely, around 6-8 inches apart.

Pruning

Regular pruning is an essential practice for maintaining good airflow in your garden:

- removing dead or crowded growth
  - Pruning involves selectively removing dead, damaged, or crowded branches and foliage from your plants. This not only enhances the overall appearance of your garden but also improves airflow by eliminating obstructions.

- enhancing airflow within plants
  - Proper pruning encourages healthier growth by allowing air to move freely within the plant's canopy. This helps prevent the buildup of moisture on leaves, reducing the risk of fungal diseases.

- encouraging fruit production
  - Pruning fruit-bearing plants, such as tomatoes and fruit trees, can redirect energy to fruit production rather than excessive foliage. This results in larger and more abundant harvests.

- timing
  - Pruning should be performed during the appropriate times for each plant species. Some plants benefit from pruning in late winter or early spring before new growth begins, while others may require ongoing maintenance throughout the growing season.

- pruning tools
  - Use sharp and clean pruning tools, such as hand pruners or pruning shears, to make clean cuts and minimize damage to plants. Always sanitize your tools between plants to prevent the spread of diseases.

Maintaining good airflow in your garden through proper plant spacing and regular pruning is essential for preventing disease, promoting healthy growth, and ensuring a bountiful harvest. By following recommended spacing guidelines and employing appropriate pruning techniques, you can create an environment where your plants thrive and enjoy optimal air circulation.

In conclusion, understanding your gardening space is the foundational step in embarking on a successful and fulfilling gardening journey. It is akin to knowing the canvas upon which you will create your masterpiece. By comprehensively assessing your backyard's unique characteristics, including sunlight, shade, and soil, you set the stage for a garden that not only survives but thrives.

Sunlight, the lifeblood of your garden, must be mapped and strategically utilized to ensure each plant receives the ideal amount of light for its growth. Soil, the bedrock of your garden's health, demands careful attention to drainage, composition, and the presence of earthworms to create a fertile and nurturing environment for your plants.

Choosing the right spot for your garden involves considering convenience, water accessibility, expansion potential, and protection against wildlife and pests. Proximity to your home fosters a stronger connection with your garden and ensures timely care and harvest. Easy access to resources and water saves you time and energy, while future expansion planning maintains your garden's integrity.

Lastly, safeguarding your garden through thoughtful design elements, like fencing and natural pest deterrents, and ensuring proper airflow through plant spacing and pruning techniques, promotes not only plant health but also a thriving ecosystem.

By mastering these aspects of understanding your space, you embark on a gardening journey that is informed, strategic, and ultimately rewarding. Your garden becomes a reflection of your care, dedication, and harmony with the natural world, a space where beauty and abundance flourish.

CHAPTER 2:

Planning Your Garden

N ow that we have a better understanding of our garden space, it's time for you to set the stage for a thriving and visually stunning outdoor oasis. In this chapter, we will delve into the essential aspects of planning your garden, from setting clear goals and objectives to designing a layout that combines functionality and aesthetics.

Setting Clear Goals and Objectives

When planning your garden, it's essential to begin with clear goals and objectives in mind. This step will provide a solid foundation for the rest of your planning process. You can use the below points as a framework in order to help you plan and achieve your gardening goals.

Define Your Purpose

Start by identifying the main purpose of your garden. Are you looking to grow your own vegetables, create a relaxing outdoor space, attract pollinators, or showcase ornamental plants? Understanding your primary goal will help you make informed decisions throughout the planning process.

Consider Your Needs

Think about what you and your family need from the garden. Are you interested in growing specific crops to supplement your meals, reduce grocery costs, or simply enjoy the taste of homegrown produce? Do you want a space for outdoor dining, relaxation, or recreation? Clearly defining your needs ensures that your garden serves its intended purpose.

Set Priorities

Sometimes, your garden goals may conflict due to limited space or resources. Setting priorities helps you determine what's most important. For example, if you have a small backyard, you might prioritize vegetable beds over a large ornamental garden.

Budget and Resources

Assess your budget and available resources, including time and energy. Gardening can be both financially and physically demanding, so it's crucial to align your goals with what you can realistically manage. I would, however, also add that even though gardening can become an expensive hobby, there are numerous different ways to garden on a budget.

Plant Selection

Selecting the right plants is a fundamental aspect of garden planning. Including the types of plants you want to grow in your plan will give a clear idea of the resources you are going to need and what to budget for.

- native vs. non-native
  - Consider whether you want to focus on native plants, which are well-suited to your local climate and support local wildlife, or if you're open to growing non-native species.
  - Native plants often require less maintenance and can promote biodiversity.

- edible vs. ornamental
  - Decide whether you want to grow edible crops, ornamental plants, or a combination of both.
  - Edible gardening can provide fresh produce, while ornamental plants enhance the aesthetics of your garden.
  - I highly recommend growing both as there are ornamental plants that can help with pest management.

- microclimates
  - Assess your garden's microclimates, including areas of sun, shade, and wind exposure.

- ○ Different plants have specific light and soil requirements, so matching them to the right microclimate is crucial for their health and productivity.

- companion planting

  - ○ Explore companion planting strategies to maximize plant health and yield.

  - ○ Some plants benefit from being grown alongside specific companions that deter pests or enhance nutrient uptake.

By keeping these points in mind, you will be able to create a clearer picture of what your garden is going to look like and all the possibilities there are.

Yield Expectations

We all want the most out of our gardens and maximizing the yield from your garden involves careful planning:

- crop selection

  - ○ Choose crops based on your preferences and available space.

  - ○ Some plants, like tomatoes, require more space, while others, like herbs, can be grown in smaller areas.

- crop rotation

  - Plan for crop rotation to maintain soil health and reduce the risk of pests and diseases.

  - Avoid planting the same type of crop in the same spot year after year.

- succession planting

  - Implement succession planting to ensure a continuous harvest.

  - This technique involves planting new crops as soon as the previous ones are harvested to make the most of your growing season.

Garden Layout

With the previous points in mind, creating a well-thought-out garden layout ensures that your outdoor space is both functional and visually appealing.

Zoning

Divide your garden into zones based on function. For example, you might have a vegetable garden zone, a relaxation zone with seating and decorative elements, and a play area for children. Zoning helps organize the space efficiently.

Traffic Flow

Plan pathways and walkways to provide easy access to different areas of the garden. Ensure that paths are wide enough for comfortable movement and consider using materials like gravel, pavers, or stepping stones.

Focal Points

Incorporate focal points in your garden design, such as a beautifully planted tree, a water feature, or a well-placed sculpture. Focal points draw the eye and create visual interest.

Plant Groupings

Group plants with similar water and care requirements together. This simplifies maintenance and helps ensure that plants thrive.

Seasonal Interest

Plan for year-round interest by selecting plants that offer different colors, textures, and bloom times throughout the seasons.

Garden Structures

Decide if you want to include structures like trellises, pergolas, or raised beds. These elements can add vertical interest and functionality to your garden.

Sketching and Planning Software

Visualizing your garden layout can help greatly for effective planning. Here are a few tips and tricks you can use:

- paper sketches
  - Sketching your garden on paper allows you to create a rough layout, experiment with different arrangements, and jot down notes.

- It's a simple and accessible way to start planning.

- garden planning software

  - Consider using specialized garden planning software or apps.

  - These tools often come with pre-loaded plant libraries, allowing you to arrange and visualize your garden digitally.

  - They can also calculate plant spacing and provide planting schedules.

- virtual reality (VR)

  - For a more immersive experience, some garden enthusiasts use VR tools to walk through their garden designs in a virtual environment before implementing them in real life.

Aesthetic Vision

Creating a garden with a consistent aesthetic vision adds beauty and character to your outdoor space.

Style Exploration

Take time to explore different garden styles, such as English cottage gardens, Japanese Zen gardens, or modern minimalist designs. Each style has its unique characteristics and can evoke distinct moods.

Color Schemes

Consider color schemes that resonate with your personal taste. Harmonious color combinations can create a cohesive and visually pleasing garden.

Texture and Contrast

Think about the texture of plants and hardscape elements in your garden. Mixing textures and creating contrast can add depth and interest to the design.

Furniture and Decor

Choose outdoor furniture and decor that align with your chosen garden style. These elements contribute to the overall aesthetic and functionality of your garden.

Seasonal Changes

Plan for how your garden's aesthetic will evolve throughout the seasons. Different plants and design elements may come to the forefront during different times of the year.

Maintenance

Consider the level of maintenance your chosen aesthetic requires. Some styles, like formal gardens, may require more upkeep, while others, like naturalistic gardens, can be more low-maintenance.

By setting clear goals and objectives, selecting the right plants, carefully planning your garden layout, managing yield expectations, and nurturing an aesthetic vision, you can create a garden that is not only functional but also a beautiful reflection of your preferences and aspirations. Gardening is an evolving process, so remain open to adjustments and enjoy the journey as your garden transforms over time.

Journal or Tracker

Maintaining a gardening journal or tracker is a valuable practice that can significantly enhance your gardening success. Here's an expanded explanation of why recording observations, dates, weather conditions, interventions, growth tracking, problem-solving, and experimentation are essential components of this journal.

Observations

1. State of your plants

   Regularly observing the condition of your plants allows you to detect early signs of stress, disease, or pest infestations. Timely intervention is often the key to preventing or mitigating damage.

2. Changes in your garden

   Noting changes in your garden, such as the appearance of new weeds or the growth of neighboring trees, helps you adapt your gardening strategies accordingly. For example, you may need to adjust the amount of sunlight a particular area receives.

3. Plant responses

   Observing how your plants respond to different environmental conditions, such as changes in temperature or rainfall, provides insights into their adaptability and helps you fine-tune your care routines.

Dates

1. Seasonal patterns

    Recording dates allows you to understand seasonal patterns in your garden. You can pinpoint when specific events, like the first frost or the arrival of pollinators, typically occur, helping you make informed decisions in advance.

2. Crop planning

    Knowing when to expect harvests based on past dates helps you plan your gardening tasks more efficiently. You can also stagger plantings to ensure a continuous supply of produce.

3. Long-term trends

    Over time, tracking dates helps you identify long-term trends in your garden, such as whether certain plants consistently perform better in specific months or seasons.

Weather Conditions

1. Environmental impact

    Weather conditions have a direct impact on plant growth and health. Recording these conditions allows you to correlate plant responses with specific weather patterns. For example, you may notice that plants thrive during periods of moderate rainfall but struggle during droughts.

2. Extreme events

Noting extreme weather events, such as heavy storms or heatwaves, helps you assess their effects on your garden. This information can inform decisions about plant selection and protective measures.

Interventions

1. Effectiveness assessment

Documenting interventions, such as fertilizing or pest control, enables you to assess their effectiveness over time. You can determine which methods yield the best results and refine your gardening practices accordingly.

2. Problem tracking

When dealing with garden issues, recording interventions helps you keep track of what you've tried and what has or hasn't worked. It prevents you from repeating unsuccessful strategies and guides you toward more effective solutions.

3. Consistency

Consistently implementing interventions and recording them ensures that you maintain a structured and organized approach to garden care. This is especially important when dealing with ongoing issues like weed control or disease management.

Growth Tracking

1. Seedling development

   Monitoring the development of seedlings provides valuable insights into the success of your germination techniques and helps you identify any issues early on, such as poor soil quality or inadequate lighting.

2. Flowering and fruit set

   Tracking when plants begin to flower and set fruit is essential for planning harvests. It allows you to anticipate when you'll need to provide support, such as trellising or staking.

3. Harvest dates

   Documenting harvest dates helps you keep a record of when specific crops are ready for picking. This information assists in planning meals and preserving excess produce.

4. Growth milestones

   Recording growth milestones, such as the emergence of the first flower or the appearance of ripe fruit, adds a personal touch to your journal and serves as a source of satisfaction as you celebrate your garden's achievements.

Problem-Solving

1. Challenges identification

   Thorough documentation of garden challenges and pest issues helps you identify patterns and potential underlying causes. It aids in preventing recurrent problems.

2. Solutions tracking

By recording the solutions and interventions you implement, you create a reference guide for future encounters with similar issues. This can save you time and effort in finding effective remedies.

3. Success rates

Tracking the success rates of your interventions provides valuable feedback on what works and what doesn't in your specific garden environment. It informs your decision-making and allows you to tailor your approach.

Experimentation

1. Customized strategies

Experimenting with different pest control methods or gardening techniques within your journal allows you to customize your strategies. Over time, you'll refine your approach based on your observations and the results you achieve.

2. Learning from experience

Your journal becomes a repository of knowledge gained from hands-on experience. You'll gain insights into your garden's unique quirks and requirements, making you a more skilled and knowledgeable gardener.

A gardening journal or tracker is a dynamic tool that evolves with your garden. It serves as a reference guide, a problem-solving resource, and a source of inspiration. By diligently recording observations, dates, weather conditions, interventions, growth tracking, and experimentation, you'll not only improve your gardening skills but also deepen your connection to your garden and the natural world. Over time, your journal becomes an invaluable companion on your gardening journey.

Project-Based Goals

Just like with the rest of life, having specific and actionable goals for your garden will only set you up for further success. To effectively achieve your gardening goals, it's crucial to break them down into specific and actionable steps. For example, if you want to create a new flower bed, outline the detailed process:

1. Select the location and size of the flower bed.

2. Prepare the soil by removing weeds and improving its quality.

3. Choose suitable plants based on sunlight and soil conditions.

4. Purchase or propagate the chosen plants.

5. Arrange and plant the flowers according to your design.

6. Mulch the bed to retain moisture and deter weeds.

7. Set up an irrigation system if necessary.

8. Establish a maintenance routine, including watering, fertilizing, and deadheading.

Transforming each gardening project into a checklist of tasks provides a clear roadmap for completing the goal. You can use various tools to create and manage these checklists, such as digital task management apps, physical notebooks, or dedicated gardening journals. Checking off completed tasks not only keeps you organized but also provides a sense of accomplishment.

You can take this even a few steps further by giving yourself a deadline, tracking your progress, and keeping to a schedule.

Deadlines

Setting realistic deadlines is essential for project-based goals. Consider the complexity of the project, your availability, seasonal factors, and the resources or assistance required. For instance, building a garden shed might take longer than planting a row of vegetables, so allocate time accordingly.

Seasonal Considerations

Recognize that some gardening tasks are best performed during specific seasons. For example, planning to start your compost pile in the fall when you have an abundance of fallen leaves is more practical than attempting it in the winter when the ground is frozen.

Scheduling

Develop a comprehensive gardening schedule that spans the entire season. Include project deadlines and milestones, planting dates, maintenance tasks, and harvest times. A well-organized schedule helps you prioritize and allocate time for different gardening activities, ensuring that they align with your overall goals.

As you achieve your gardening goals, don't forget to celebrate them— you deserve it. Celebrate your gardening milestones, no matter how small they may seem. Completing projects and reaching goals should be acknowledged and appreciated. Recognizing your achievements boosts motivation and fosters a sense of accomplishment, encouraging you to continue working toward your objectives.

Maintain a gardening journal or tracker to record the completion of each project-based goal. Note the date when you finished the task and any observations about the results. This documentation becomes a valuable reference for future gardening endeavors and allows you to reflect on your progress over time.

You could also consider taking photographs before and after each project. Visual documentation provides a tangible record of your gardening journey's evolution. These photos serve as inspiration and help you track the improvements you've made, offering a visual representation of your accomplishments.

Incorporating project-based goals into your gardening plan not only makes your tasks more manageable but also enhances your gardening experience. It allows you to approach your garden projects systematically and efficiently. Setting realistic deadlines keeps you accountable and ensures that you stay on track throughout the gardening season. Celebrating achievements and documenting progress makes your gardening journey more rewarding and provides a tangible record of your growth as a gardener.

Strategic-Based Goals

With the same determination you tackle your projects, why not incorporate the same mindset towards the rest of your gardening journey? Adopt strategic gardening goals and tactics to further assist you. These goals encompass a holistic approach to gardening that goes beyond planting and maintenance. They involve thoughtful practices aimed at enhancing soil health, promoting environmental stewardship, and ensuring your garden can thrive year-round. Let's delve into some of these core principles and practices of strategic-based gardening, including self-sustaining garden strategies, year-round gardening techniques, and environmentally conscious practices. You can cultivate a self-sustaining garden that gives you produce year-round and become an environmental steward by incorporating the following 12 goals into your gardening endeavors. You'll not only nurture your plants but also cultivate a garden that harmonizes with the natural world and yields bountiful rewards.

Self-Sustaining Garden

An excellent gardening goal for the long term is to have a self-sustaining garden. This reduces the amount of work and maintenance you have to do and can increase your edible harvests.

1. Crop rotations

   Crop rotation is the method of systematically planting various crops in the same garden beds or areas over multiple seasons. This approach serves to disrupt the life cycles of pests and diseases that target specific plant families while also preventing soil exhaustion by adjusting the nutrient requirements of different crops. For instance, after growing tomatoes in a particular bed one season, one might choose to plant beans there the following season to rejuvenate nitrogen levels in the soil.

2. Companion planting

    Companion planting, on the other hand, is a strategy in which specific plants are cultivated together to enhance their mutual growth, discourage pests, or facilitate pollination. For instance, the act of planting basil near tomatoes can deter aphids, while the inclusion of marigolds alongside vegetables can repel nematodes. Companion planting helps to reduce the necessity for chemical pesticides and promotes a healthier garden ecosystem.

3. Cover crops

    Cover crops, sometimes referred to as green manure, are plants grown primarily to benefit the soil rather than for harvest. These crops serve to shield the soil from erosion, suppress the growth of weeds, and enhance the overall structure of the soil. Legumes such as clover or vetch are frequently employed as cover crops because they can naturally enrich the soil by fixing nitrogen. When these cover crops are incorporated into the soil, they provide organic matter and nutrients for subsequent plantings.

4. Composting

Composting, meanwhile, is the process of converting organic matter, such as kitchen scraps, yard waste, and fallen leaves, into humus that is rich in nutrients. This humus can be incorporated into the garden soil, enhancing its structure, capacity to retain moisture, and nutrient content. Composting lessens the need for synthetic fertilizers, which can leach into groundwater and have adverse environmental effects.

5. Rainwater harvesting

Lastly, rainwater harvesting refers to the practice of collecting and storing rainwater runoff from rooftops and other surfaces. This collected rainwater can be utilized for garden irrigation, diminishing the dependence on municipal water sources. Common tools for rainwater collection include rain barrels or cisterns. By employing rainwater in this way, you conserve treated drinking water and reduce the energy required to pump water from reservoirs.

Year-Round Gardening

1. Crop selection

Year-round gardening requires careful selection of crops that can withstand different seasons. Cold-hardy vegetables and fruits, such as kale, carrots, and winter squash, can tolerate frost and low temperatures, making them suitable for winter gardening. Research your specific climate and choose varieties adapted to your region.

2. Season-extending tools

   Season-extending tools like cold frames, row covers, and cloches provide protection against cold weather and extend the growing season. Cold frames act as miniature greenhouses, while row covers and cloches create microclimates that shield plants from frost. These tools allow you to grow crops earlier in the spring and later into the fall.

3. Greenhouse gardening

   Greenhouses provide a controlled environment for year-round gardening. They offer temperature and humidity control, protection from extreme weather, and the ability to grow a wide variety of crops. Greenhouse gardening is ideal for starting seeds, overwintering tender plants, and growing exotic or out-of-season crops.

4. Climate management

   Efficient climate management in greenhouses is essential for successful year-round gardening. Ventilation systems regulate temperature and humidity, preventing overheating in the summer and frost damage in the winter. Heating systems keep the greenhouse warm during cold spells, and cooling systems prevent excessive heat buildup. Monitoring tools help you maintain optimal conditions for plant growth.

Environmental Stewardship

1. Water conservation

   Water conservation practices in gardening include mulching to retain soil moisture, collecting and using rainwater, and employing efficient irrigation systems like drip irrigation. These practices minimize water waste, reduce the need for excessive watering, and help protect water resources.

2. Organic fertilizers

   Organic fertilizers, such as compost, well-rotted manure, and organic matter, release nutrients slowly and improve soil structure. They promote healthy microbial life in the soil and reduce reliance on synthetic fertilizers, which can leach into waterways and harm aquatic ecosystems.

3. Reduced chemical use

   Integrated pest management (IPM) is an approach that minimizes the use of synthetic chemicals in gardening. Instead, it focuses on biological controls like introducing beneficial insects, using traps, and practicing good garden hygiene. IPM also involves monitoring and early detection of pests and diseases to implement environmentally friendly solutions, reducing the environmental impact of chemical pesticides.

By setting and implementing strategic-based goals in your garden, you not only promote plant health but also contribute to a more sustainable and eco-friendly gardening practice. These goals encompass essential elements such as soil health, environmental impact reduction, and creating a resilient, self-sustaining garden capable of year-round productivity.

Remember that successful gardening is a dynamic journey that involves ongoing learning and adaptation. Stay open to adjusting your goals and strategies based on your experiences and evolving interests and you'll continue to enjoy the rewards of your sustainable garden.

CHAPTER 3:
Essential Gardening Tools

G ardening is an exciting adventure, and like any journey, you need the right tools and supplies to get started. In this chapter, we'll get down and dirty to equip you with essential gardening tools and guide you through selecting top-quality soil, fertilizers, and seeds to ensure your garden thrives.

Must-Have Tools for Beginners

Picture yourself as a gardening superhero, armed with an array of essential tools, poised to conquer any horticultural challenge that comes your way. To embark on your green-thumbed journey with confidence, you'll want to ensure your gardening utility belt is well-stocked with these must-have tools, specially tailored for beginners:

1. Hand trowel

    Think of the hand trowel as your trusty sidekick in the garden. This compact and versatile tool excels at planting, digging, and transplanting. Consider it the Swiss Army knife of gardening, always at your disposal for those precision tasks.

2. Pruners or secateurs

   Pruning is an art, and your pruners are the brushstrokes that help you create the perfect garden painting. These essential tools allow you to trim and shape your plants, promoting healthy growth and a tidy appearance.

3. Garden gloves

   Protect your hands from the perils of thorns, dirt, and blisters with a reliable pair of garden gloves. They're your armor, ensuring that your hands remain safe and comfortable as you venture through your garden.

4. Garden fork

   The garden fork is your go-to implement for soil aeration, breaking up clumps, and turning compost. This powerhouse tool is pivotal in maintaining soil health and ensuring your plants thrive.

5. Watering can or hose

   Your plants are thirstier than you might imagine, and you'll need a dependable watering can or hose to quench their hydration needs. Be sure it allows you to reach every nook and cranny of your garden.

6. Garden rake

   Whether you're leveling soil, clearing debris, or creating smooth seedbeds, a garden rake is your versatile assistant. It's the key to keeping your garden's appearance neat and orderly.

7. Wheelbarrow

   Gardening frequently involves transporting hefty loads like soil, mulch, or plants. A wheelbarrow becomes your trusty companion, sparing your back and simplifying the movement of materials.

8. Pruning saw

   For those thicker branches and overgrown shrubs, a pruning saw is an indispensable tool. Its sharp teeth allow you to make clean cuts and shape woody plants with precision.

9. Garden kneeler and seat

   Gardening is a physically demanding task, often taking a toll on your knees and back. Invest in a garden kneeler and seat that offers both comfort and support as you work close to the ground.

10. Garden hat and sunscreen

    Don't overlook your personal protection while nurturing your garden. A wide-brimmed garden hat and sunscreen act as your armor against the sun's rays, ensuring your comfort and safety.

Now that you've assembled your gardening toolkit, it's time to transition to the heart of your garden: the soil, fertilizers, and seeds. These foundational elements will pave the way for your gardening journey, transforming your outdoor space into a thriving oasis of greenery.

Selecting Quality Soil, Fertilizers, and Seeds

Your garden's success hinges on the soil you use, the fertilizers you apply, and the seeds you sow. These fundamental elements form the bedrock of your gardening journey. Let's delve into each component with a discerning eye.

Things to Look For

Soil

When perusing soil options, consider its texture, pH level, and drainage capacity. The gold standard is loamy soil with a neutral pH of around 6.5 and excellent drainage as it suits most plants. However, tailor your soil choice to the specific needs of the plants you plan to cultivate.

Fertilizers

Fertilizers are the lifeblood of plant nutrition. To make informed choices, gauge your plants' nutritional requirements. Look for balanced nitrogen, phosphorus, and potassium (NPK) ratios on fertilizer labels. Organic options, such as compost or well-rotted manure, enrich the soil naturally and improve its structure.

Seeds

The seeds you select can significantly influence your garden's triumph. Opt for seeds from reputable suppliers or esteemed seed banks. Scrutinize the information provided on seed packets encompassing planting depth, spacing, and germination times.

Top Three Products

Navigating the plethora of products at your local gardening store can be a daunting task. To streamline your decision-making process, here are the top three recommendations for each category:

Soil

1. Potting mix

   If you're venturing into container gardening, a premium potting mix is your go-to choice. It boasts exceptional drainage and aeration, ensuring your potted plants flourish.

2. Garden soil

   For raised beds and in-ground planting, opt for a versatile garden soil. Seek out options enriched with compost to provide your plants with additional nutrients.

3. Compost

   Incorporating compost into your soil is an exemplary approach to enhancing fertility. You can either acquire bagged compost or embark on the rewarding journey of creating your own by composting kitchen scraps and yard waste.

Fertilizers

1. All-purpose organic fertilizer

   An organic fertilizer with balanced NPK ratios (e.g., 5-5-5) is a versatile choice that caters to most plants' essential nutrient needs. It suits a wide array of gardening endeavors.

2. Fish emulsion

    Fish emulsion, a natural liquid fertilizer brimming with nutrients, facilitates rapid nutrient absorption by plants. It's particularly advantageous for fast-growing crops.

3. Bone meal

    Bone meal serves as an outstanding source of phosphorus, fostering root development and flowering in plants. It's especially valuable for flowering plants and bulbs.

Seeds

1. Heirloom seeds

    For gardeners with a penchant for unique and traditional plant varieties, heirloom seeds are the ideal selection. They offer genetic diversity and authentic flavors, catering to those who relish culinary experimentation.

2. Hybrid seeds

    Renowned for their reliability and disease resistance, hybrid seeds are an excellent choice for novices seeking bountiful yields and minimal maintenance.

3. Organic seeds

    If you're devoted to eco-friendly gardening practices, certified organic seeds are a requisite. These seeds originate from plants cultivated without synthetic pesticides or fertilizers, aligning seamlessly with sustainable gardening principles.

By carefully considering your soil, fertilizer, and seed choices, you lay a sturdy foundation for your garden's prosperity. With the right components in place, your garden will thrive, bearing witness to the beauty of nature's growth and abundance.

DIY Soil and Fertilizers

If you're a hands-on gardener with a penchant for personalization, creating your own soil mix and fertilizers is a rewarding endeavor. This approach allows you to craft gardening elements that cater specifically to your garden's unique requirements. Here's a brief step-by-step guide for each. You'll find an in-depth step-by-step guide in the next Chapter.

DIY Soil Mix

1. Gather ingredients.

    A. Start by assembling organic materials that will enhance your soil's structure, aeration, and moisture retention.

    B. You'll want to collect items such as compost, peat moss, perlite, and vermiculite.

2. Measure and mix.

    A. Employ a large container or wheelbarrow to measure and combine your chosen ingredients.

    B. A typical mix might consist of equal parts compost, peat moss, and perlite.

3. Blend thoroughly.

    A. Blend the ingredients diligently until you achieve a consistent and well-mixed soil medium.

    B. It's vital that all components are evenly distributed, ensuring uniform soil quality throughout.

DIY Organic Fertilizer

1. Collect ingredients.

    A. Begin by accumulating a variety of organic materials including kitchen scraps like fruit and vegetable peels, coffee grounds, eggshells, and yard waste such as grass clippings and leaves.

2. Layer ingredients.

    A. Create layers within a compost pile or bin, alternating between green materials (kitchen scraps, grass clippings) and brown materials (leaves, cardboard). Green layers supply nitrogen, while brown layers offer carbon.

3. Turn the pile.

    A. To encourage decomposition and facilitate microbial activity, routinely turn the compost pile. As time passes, these microorganisms will break down the materials, transforming them into nutrient-rich compost.

By embarking on the journey of crafting your own soil mix and fertilizers, you gain the advantage of fine-tuning these crucial elements to align precisely with your garden's distinct requirements. This hands-on approach empowers you to create the ideal environment for your plants to flourish.

In conclusion, as you embark on your gardening odyssey, ensure you arm yourself with the right tools and the knowledge to select top-quality soil, fertilizers, and seeds. Armed with this information and your newfound DIY expertise, you're well-equipped to cultivate a flourishing garden that will grace you with exquisite blooms and abundant harvests. It's time to roll up your sleeves, don your gardening gloves, and transform your backyard into a thriving haven of natural beauty and productivity!

CHAPTER 4:

Preparing the Soil

W
e had some brief looks into the soil in the previous chapters, but because the soil in your garden is so important, we need to dig deeper and have a look at the different soil types. You must also know how to identify, test the pH, and amend these different soil types. As not all plants like the same type of soil, it is important to know what type you are dealing with.

Different Soil Types

Understanding different soil types is essential for successful gardening because it affects water retention, drainage, nutrient availability, and plant health. Here's an in-depth look at the main soil types you may encounter in your garden:

Loam Soil

Loam soil is often considered the ideal soil type for gardening. It's a balanced mixture of sand, silt, and clay, with each component making up approximately 30% of the soil composition.

Characteristics

- *Well-draining*: Loam soil allows water to drain efficiently, preventing waterlogged roots.

- *Holds moisture*: It retains adequate moisture for plants to access between waterings.

- *Nutrient-rich*: Loam soil typically contains a good balance of nutrients, making it suitable for a wide range of plants.

Best for

Most vegetables, flowers, and shrubs thrive in loam soil. This would be the best soil type if you plan on growing a wide variety of different plant types.

Sandy Soil

Sandy soil consists of large, coarse particles with low silt and clay content. It feels gritty to the touch.

Characteristics

- *Fast-draining*: Sandy soil drains rapidly, which can lead to frequent watering requirements.

- *Low moisture retention:* It struggles to retain moisture and nutrients, making it less suitable for some plants.

- *Easy to work with*: Sandy soil is easy to till and cultivate due to its loose texture.

Best for
Plants that prefer well-drained conditions, such as succulents, carrots, and onions.

Clay Soil
Clay soil is composed of fine particles and has a smooth, sticky texture when wet. It compacts easily and becomes hard when dry.

Characteristics
- *Poor drainage*: Clay soil drains slowly and can become waterlogged.

- *Excellent nutrient retention*: It holds onto nutrients well, making them available to plants.

- *Susceptible to compaction*: Clay soil can become hard and compacted, limiting root growth.

Best for
Plants that don't mind moisture retention, such as water-loving vegetables like rice and watercress.

Silt Soil
Silt soil consists of fine particles that are smaller than sand but larger than clay. It feels smooth and retains moisture better than sandy soil.

Characteristics
- *Holds moisture*: Silt soil retains moisture well, making it suitable for many plant types.

- *Prone to compaction*: Like clay, silt soil can become compacted, which can restrict root growth and water infiltration.

- *Nutrient-rich*: Silt soil contains a good amount of nutrients.

Best for

A wide variety of plants, including vegetables, herbs, and flowers.

Peat Soil

Peat soil is composed mainly of partially decayed organic matter, particularly sphagnum moss. It has a very high organic content—think potting soil or organic soil that you buy from the store.

Characteristics

- *Excellent moisture retention*: Peat soil retains water exceptionally well but can become waterlogged.

- *Acidic pH*: It tends to be acidic, which may require pH adjustment for certain plants.

- *Low in nutrients*: Peat soil lacks essential nutrients, so supplemental fertilization is often necessary.

Best for

Acid-loving plants like blueberries and camellias and as a component in potting mixes.

Chalky or Alkaline Soil

Chalky soil contains a high level of calcium carbonate and has an alkaline pH.

Characteristics

- *Excellent drainage*: Chalky soil drains well but can lead to nutrient deficiencies.

- *Alkaline pH*: The high pH may limit the availability of certain nutrients to plants.

- *May require amendments*: Some plants may struggle in chalky soil and benefit from pH adjustment and nutrient supplementation.

Best for

Alkaline-tolerant plants like lavender and lilacs or for amending acidic soil to accommodate specific crops.

Understanding your soil type and its characteristics is critical to selecting the right plants, making appropriate amendments, and maintaining a healthy garden. Soil testing can provide valuable insights into your soil's composition and help you make informed decisions for your garden.

Soil Testing and Amendments

Conducting a DIY soil test is a fundamental skill for any gardener. It provides insight into your soil's composition and pH, enabling you to make informed decisions about amendments and plant selection. Let's break down the process:

Step-By-Step Soil Testing

1. Acquire a soil test kit.

   Soil test kits are available at most gardening centers and online stores. These kits typically include pH testing strips, color-coded charts for interpretation, and instructions.

   Some advanced kits may also offer additional tests for essential nutrients like nitrogen, phosphorus, and potassium (NPK).

2. Collect representative soil samples.

   A. Before collecting soil samples, ensure your tools are clean and free from contaminants. Use a stainless steel trowel or soil probe for accuracy.

   B. Choose several locations throughout your garden, particularly areas where you plan to grow different types of plants or where you suspect soil variations.

   C. Remove any surface debris or organic matter and dig a small hole or trench at each selected site, ensuring a depth of 6 to 8 inches.

   D. Using a clean container, collect soil samples from each hole, taking care to avoid touching the soil with your hands.

E. Combine the collected samples in a clean bucket and mix them thoroughly to create a composite sample that represents your entire garden area.

3. Test pH levels.

A. Follow the kit's instructions to test the pH of your soil.

B. Typically, you'll mix a small portion of your composite sample with water to create a slurry.

C. Insert the pH testing strip into the slurry and compare the resulting color to the chart provided with the testing kit. The color change will indicate the pH level, which can range from acidic (below 7), neutral (around 7), to alkaline (above 7).

D. Interpret the results to determine your soil's acidity or alkalinity.

Interpretation of the Results

Understanding your soil's pH is crucial as different plants have specific pH preferences. For example, most vegetables prefer slightly acidic to neutral soil (pH 6.0–7.0), while blueberries thrive in acidic soil (pH 4.5–5.5).

To interpret the results, you need to understand your specific plants' pH preferences. Here are some general guidelines you can follow:

- slightly acidic to neutral (pH 6.0-7.0)

    o This range is suitable for many common garden vegetables, flowers, and shrubs.

- acidic (pH 4.5-5.5)

    o Acidic soil is preferred by plants like blueberries, azaleas, and rhododendrons.

- alkaline (pH above 7.0)

    o Some plants, such as lilacs and asparagus, thrive in slightly alkaline soil.

If your soil falls outside the optimal pH range for your desired plants, you'll need to make amendments to adjust the pH accordingly. Before we get into how to amend your garden soil, let's first look at another option for testing the soil.

Professional Soil Testing

While DIY tests provide valuable insights, professional soil testing offers a more comprehensive analysis of your soil's composition.

Here's how to go about it:

- local agricultural extension offices

    o Contact your local agricultural extension office, which often provides soil testing services.

    o These offices are usually affiliated with universities and offer affordable or even free soil testing.

- They will provide you with specific instructions on how to collect and submit soil samples.

- collecting samples for professional testing
  - Typically, you'll follow the same collection process as for DIY testing.

  - Ensure you collect samples from representative areas of your garden to obtain accurate results.

  - Label each sample container with the corresponding location and any relevant information about the plants you plan to grow in that area.

- submitting samples
  - Deliver or send your soil samples to the designated laboratory or office.

  - Include any required forms, payment if applicable, and any specific information they request.

  - Wait for the results, which may take a few weeks depending on the lab's workload.

Soil testing is a valuable tool that helps identify nutrient deficiencies or imbalances in your soil. It provides specific information about your soil's nutrient content, pH level, and other factors that affect plant growth. For example, if your soil test reveals a lack of phosphorus, your plants may struggle to develop strong root systems and may have difficulty producing flowers or fruits.

Understanding what nutrients your soil needs and why it needs them is crucial for successful gardening. Here's a more detailed explanation of nutrient considerations and choosing the right amendments.

Common Nutrients (NPK)

Nitrogen (N)

Nitrogen is essential for promoting lush foliage and vigorous vegetative growth in plants. It plays a vital role in the production of chlorophyll, the green pigment responsible for photosynthesis.

Phosphorus (P)

Phosphorus supports root development, flowering, and fruiting. It's particularly critical during the early stages of plant growth when root systems are being established and later during flowering and fruit production.

Potassium (K)

Potassium enhances overall plant health, including disease resistance and stress tolerance. It helps regulate water uptake and nutrient movement within the plant.

Depending on the results of your soil test, you can select appropriate amendments to rectify nutrient deficiencies. Here are a few examples:

Organic Amendments

Organic materials like compost and well-rotted manure are excellent choices. They not only provide essential nutrients but also improve soil structure, water retention, and microbial activity. Organic amendments contribute to long-term soil health and fertility.

Fertilizers

If your soil test indicates specific nutrient deficiencies, you can choose fertilizers with balanced NPK ratios. These fertilizers provide targeted nutrients, helping to address deficiencies efficiently.

Lime or Sulfur

Adjusting soil pH is another important aspect of soil management. If your soil is too acidic (low pH) or too alkaline (high pH) for your desired plants, you can use lime to raise pH or elemental sulfur to lower it.

Micronutrient Supplements

In addition to the primary macronutrients (NPK), plants require trace elements, also known as micronutrients, such as iron, manganese, and zinc. If your soil lacks these micronutrients, you can apply specific supplements as needed.

Conducting soil tests, whether you do it yourself or seek professional assistance, is a fundamental step in gardening. It empowers you to make informed decisions about soil amendments, ensuring that your plants receive the necessary nutrients to thrive.

Understanding the roles of pH levels and nutrient requirements is key to cultivating a vibrant and productive garden, ultimately leading to healthier and more bountiful plants.

Creating a Fertile and Healthy Soil

Once you've conducted a soil test and identified any pH or nutrient imbalances, it's time to take action and create a fertile and healthy soil environment for your plants. Let's dive deeper into soil pH, amendments, and how to create healthy and fertile soil for your garden.

How to Balance Soil

Balancing soil pH is crucial because it directly affects nutrient availability to plants.

For Acidic Soils (Low pH)

- Apply lime.
  - Lime, in the form of ground limestone, is a common amendment to raise pH levels in acidic soils.
  - It effectively neutralizes acidity and makes the soil more alkaline.
- Apply dolomite lime.
  - If your soil is both acidic and deficient in magnesium, dolomite lime is a suitable choice as it addresses both issues.

For Alkaline Soils (High pH)

- Amend with sulfur.

    o Elemental sulfur is a common choice for lowering pH in alkaline soils.

    o It converts to sulfuric acid when broken down by soil bacteria, gradually reducing alkalinity.

- Add peat moss.

    o Incorporating peat moss can also lower soil pH.

    o It adds organic matter, increases acidity, and improves moisture retention.

Organic Matter Incorporation

Enhancing your soil's structure and nutrient content is essential for overall plant health. To do so the best way is to incorporate organic matter into the soil. There are a number of different ways you can do this but let's look at the top three:

- compost

    o Incorporate compost into your soil to improve its organic matter content.

    o Compost enhances soil structure, moisture retention, and nutrient availability.

- well-rotted manure
  - Aged or well-rotted manure adds valuable nutrients and beneficial microorganisms to the soil and it also improves soil structure.

- cover crops
  - Planting cover crops, such as legumes or clover, during the off-season can further enrich the soil.
  - These crops fix nitrogen, prevent erosion, and add organic matter when turned under the soil.

Organic amendments provide long-term benefits to soil health and sustainability. Bagged compost is available at garden centers or can be made at home. It enriches the soil with organic matter and essential nutrients. Some garden centers may also offer well-rotted manure for purchase. It's a valuable source of nutrients and improves soil structure.

- fish emulsion, bone meal, and other organic fertilizers
  - These organic fertilizers can be found at garden stores and provide specific nutrients required by plants.

- synthetic fertilizers
  - Synthetic fertilizers are readily available and come in various formulations designed for specific plant needs. They offer precise control over nutrient content.

o   Look for fertilizers with NPK ratios that match your soil test recommendations.

o   Follow package instructions for application rates and timing.

Retesting Soil

Soil conditions change over time due to factors like plant uptake, weather, and microbial activity. To maintain a healthy and balanced soil environment, retesting is essential. Ideally, retest your soil every two to three years to monitor nutrient levels and pH. Retesting is particularly crucial if you notice any decline in plant health, nutrient deficiencies, or pH imbalances.

When retesting, follow the same collection process as your initial test:

1.   Collect samples from various areas of your garden to ensure representation.

2.   Label the samples accurately to track changes in specific areas.

By balancing your soil's pH and incorporating organic matter, you provide an ideal foundation for your plants to thrive. Regular retesting ensures your soil remains in optimal condition, and by sourcing nutrients from reliable sources, you can support healthy and vibrant plant growth in your garden.

How to Mix Your Own Organic Garden Soil

Mixing your own organic garden soil allows you to tailor the composition to your specific plant needs and ensures a healthy, nutrient-rich environment for your garden.

Here's a step-by-step guide on how to mix your own organic garden soil:

Materials You'll Need

1. Compost

    A. High-quality compost is the foundation of organic soil. It provides essential nutrients and improves soil structure.

    B. You can purchase bagged compost or make your own.

2. Peat moss

    A. Peat moss enhances moisture retention and helps loosen the soil. It's particularly useful if you have heavy clay soil.

3. Vermiculite or perlite

    A. Vermiculite and perlite are lightweight materials that improve soil aeration and drainage. They prevent compaction and root rot.

4. Well-rotted manure

    A. Aged or well-rotted manure adds valuable nutrients to your soil. Ensure it's fully composted to avoid burning your plants.

5. Organic matter

   A. Besides compost, you can add other organic matter like leaf mold, shredded leaves, or straw to further enrich the soil.

6. Garden lime or sulfur

   A. Depending on your soil's pH test results, you may need to adjust the pH. Garden lime raises pH in acidic soils, while sulfur lowers pH in alkaline soils.

Steps to Mix Your Own Organic Garden Soil

1. Determine your soil needs.

   a. Before mixing, conduct a soil test to identify pH levels and nutrient deficiencies.

   b. Based on the test results, determine if you need to adjust the pH and which nutrients are lacking.

2. Calculate the volume.

   B. Measure the area of your garden bed in square feet and calculate the volume you'll need to fill it to your desired depth (usually 6-12 inches).

3. Prepare the ingredients.

   a. Purchase or gather the necessary ingredients in the right quantities based on your calculations.

   b. If you're using garden lime or sulfur for pH adjustment, follow the recommended rates on the packaging.

4. Mix the soil.

    a. In a large container, wheelbarrow, or directly in your garden bed, combine the ingredients in the following ratios:

        i. 50-60% compost: This forms the bulk of your soil and provides nutrients.

        ii. 20-30% peat moss: Improves moisture retention and soil structure.

        iii. 10-20% vermiculite or perlite: Enhances drainage and aeration.

        iv. 5-10% well-rotted manure: Adds additional nutrients.

        v. 5-10% other organic matter: Provides further enrichment.

5. Thoroughly mix.

    a. Use a shovel or garden fork to thoroughly mix the ingredients. Aim for an even distribution throughout the soil.

6. Adjust pH (if needed).

    a. If your soil test indicates a need for pH adjustment, apply garden lime to raise pH or sulfur to lower pH based on the recommended rates.

7. Test and adjust.

    a. After mixing, it's a good practice to retest the soil's pH and nutrient levels to ensure they meet your plant requirements.

    b. Make any necessary adjustments based on the retest results.

8. Fill your garden bed.

    a. Transfer the freshly mixed organic soil into your garden bed, filling it to the desired depth.

9. Plant.

    a. Once your garden bed is filled, you're ready to plant your chosen crops or flowers.

Mixing your own organic garden soil allows you to create a customized, nutrient-rich environment that promotes healthy plant growth. By incorporating compost, organic matter, and appropriate amendments, you'll provide your plants with the ideal conditions to thrive. Periodic soil testing and adjustments ensure your garden soil remains in optimal health.

CHAPTER 5:
Starting Seeds and Seedlings

When it's time to plant all those plants your heart desires, there are three ways you can do it. You can either buy seeds and sow directly in the ground, start seedlings in separate containers, or you can buy seedlings. Seedlings are those young plants you see at the nurseries that have been grown in containers. All these options work great, and the choice will be based on your own personal preference and budget. Seedlings can be more expensive than seed packets, and with seeds, you get a whole lot more for the same price or cheaper.

However, I will add this: If you are in a hurry to get plants in the ground, I would suggest starting out with seedlings. This way, you cut back a couple of weeks in the growing stage, and as the plants mature and generate their own seeds, you can resow those seeds. You can basically leave some of the crops to go to seed each season and have enough seeds for the next, meaning you most likely won't have to buy seeds or seedlings again.

Starting seeds and nurturing seedlings is a crucial phase in gardening that sets the foundation for a successful garden. In this chapter, we'll explore easy step-by-step germination tips and techniques, the optimal timing for starting seedlings, and essential considerations like watering, soil selection, and container systems.

Germination Tips and Techniques

First, let's start out with how you can start your own seedlings from seeds.

It's important to purchase quality seeds from reputable suppliers and choose the right soil mix and container.

What to look for when buying seeds:

1. Reputable suppliers

   Look for well-established seed suppliers known for their quality and reliability. Reputable companies often provide detailed information about the seeds' origin, germination rates, and cultivation tips.

2. Check expiration dates

   Always check the seed packets for expiration dates. Fresh seeds generally have higher germination rates. While older seeds might still germinate, their success rate tends to decrease over time.

Of course, you will need a good seed starter soil to grow your own seedlings:

1. Fresh seed-starting mix

    A seed-starting mix is designed to be sterile, reducing the risk of soil-borne diseases that can harm seedlings.

2. Well-draining

    A good seed-starting mix has excellent drainage properties to prevent waterlogged conditions that can lead to seedling rot.

3. Lightweight

    Lightweight mixes prevent compaction, allowing delicate roots to grow easily.

Once you have your seeds and the mix you will be growing them in, it is time to choose the right container. Here are a few things you can keep in mind when container shopping.

Choosing a Container

Choosing the right containers to start seeds and grow seedlings is an important step for the health and development of your seedlings. There are a variety of different containers to choose from, such as seed trays, peat pots, recycled containers, and a whole bunch more. Let's have a look at some of these so you will be well-equipped when choosing the housing for your seedlings.

Seed Trays With Cells

Seed trays are specifically designed for seed starting and come with individual cells. Each cell provides a separate environment for a single seed or a few seeds. These trays are convenient for organization and transplanting as you can easily separate individual seedlings.

Seed trays often come with clear plastic domes that create a mini-greenhouse effect, maintaining warmth and humidity for germination.

Peat Pots or Pellets

Peat pots and pellets are biodegradable containers made from compressed peat moss. They are convenient for transplanting because you can plant them directly into the garden soil without disturbing the seedlings' roots.

Peat pots allow for air exchange and they naturally decompose in the soil over time.

Recycled Containers

You can repurpose various containers for seed starting, such as yogurt cups, egg cartons, or plastic containers with drainage holes. Ensure these containers are clean and sanitized before use to prevent disease.

Recycled containers are cost-effective but may require extra care to maintain appropriate moisture levels.

Plastic or Biodegradable Pots

Small plastic pots or biodegradable pots are suitable for seedlings that need more space to grow before transplanting. They come in various sizes and are reusable if properly cleaned.

Soil Blocks

Soil blocks are created using a specialized tool that compresses seed-starting mix into blocks. They eliminate the need for individual containers and allow seedlings to grow in a soil block that can be transplanted directly into the garden.

Soil blocks promote healthy root growth and reduce transplant shock.

Plastic Inserts and Trays

Some gardeners prefer using plastic inserts and trays, which can be filled with seed-starting mix. These are versatile and can accommodate various cell sizes and configurations.

When selecting containers, consider the space available for your seedlings, the types of plants you're growing, and your transplanting plans. Ensure that your chosen containers have proper drainage to prevent overwatering and label them to keep track of the seed varieties. Ultimately, the right containers will provide a conducive environment for seed germination and seedling growth.

Remember, when reusing containers from previous gardening endeavors, cleanliness is paramount. Before planting new seeds, thoroughly clean and sterilize containers to eliminate any potential plant or soil diseases that might be lingering from prior use.

A very important aspect, no matter what type of container you use, is proper drainage. Adequate drainage is a fundamental requirement for seedling containers. Ensure that the containers you select have drainage holes in the bottom. These holes are essential to allow excess water to escape, preventing waterlogged soil that can lead to seedling rot. Without proper drainage, your seedlings are at risk of suffering from root diseases and poor growth.

Planting Seeds and Growing Seedlings Step-By-Step

Starting seeds indoors or in a sheltered area during the cold months can give you a head start on the growing season.

Determining the timing for starting seedlings depends on your region's last expected frost date and the specific plants you intend to grow. Consult a local gardening calendar or your area's agricultural extension office to find the frost dates relevant to your location.

Generally, you should start seeds indoors 6–8 weeks before the last expected frost date for warm-season crops, such as tomatoes and peppers. For long-season varieties, like certain tomatoes and eggplants, you may start them up to 12 weeks ahead.

1. Sow seeds at the right depth

   Refer to the seed packet for specific planting depth instructions. It's crucial to provide seeds with the right conditions to germinate successfully.

2. Small vs. large seeds

   As a general guideline, smaller seeds are often sprinkled on the surface, while larger seeds may be gently pressed into the mix.

3. Moisten the mix

Achieve even moisture distribution throughout the mix by gradually adding water and thoroughly mixing. You want the mix to be consistently damp but not soaked.

4. Sow seeds evenly

Sow seeds evenly and avoid overcrowding seeds. Overcrowding can lead to competition for resources, resulting in weak and leggy seedlings. Follow the spacing recommendations on the seed packet.

5. Label containers

Labeling containers is essential, especially if you are growing multiple varieties of seeds. It helps you keep track of what you planted and when.

6. Provide warmth

Maintain a consistent temperature within the optimal range for each seed type. Some seeds may require warmer conditions than others. Using a seedling heat mat is an effective way to regulate temperature and promote germination.

7. Cover containers

Covering containers with plastic domes or wraps creates a controlled environment that retains moisture and warmth during germination.

8. Monitor closely

   Keep a close eye on the moisture levels under the cover to prevent excessive humidity or mold growth.

9. Light and ventilation

   Seedlings need bright, indirect light to grow strong and healthy. If natural light is insufficient, consider using grow lights. Adequate ventilation helps prevent fungal issues and encourages sturdy seedling growth. Ensure good air circulation by removing covers once seedlings emerge. A small fan on low can also promote air movement.

10. Avoid direct sunlight

    Avoid placing seedlings in direct sunlight as it can scorch or dry out delicate seedlings.

Following these germination tips and techniques will help ensure successful seed starting and the healthy development of your seedlings. Proper care during this early stage sets the foundation for a successful gardening season.

Sowing Seeds Directly in the Garden Soil

The other option is to sow seeds directly in the ground, but you need to wait for the last frost to pass and soil temperatures to rise.

1. Prepare the garden bed.

   When preparing your garden bed for direct seeding, ensure that it's free from weeds, debris, and any compacted soil.

Loosen the soil to a depth of about 6 inches (15 cm) to provide a loose and friable seedbed. Level the soil surface evenly.

2. Read seed packets.

   Seed packets are your invaluable guides when sowing directly in the garden. They provide critical information such as planting depth, spacing, and timing. Pay attention to these details as different plants have specific requirements.

3. Sow seeds.

   Plant your seeds at the recommended depth and spacing mentioned on the seed packets. As a general rule of thumb, plant seeds to a depth of about two to three times their diameter. Depending on the type of crop, you can create furrows, rows, or simply scatter seeds evenly across the prepared soil. After sowing, cover the seeds with soil as per the packet instructions.

4. Water gently.

   After sowing, water the area gently to settle the soil and provide the necessary moisture for germination. Use a fine mist spray bottle or a watering can with a rose attachment to avoid displacing the seeds. The goal is to provide adequate moisture without disturbing the soil surface.

5. Mulch and monitor.

   Applying a thin layer of mulch over the planted area helps conserve moisture, regulate soil temperature, and prevent soil erosion. Keep a close eye on the soil's moisture level, especially during the critical germination period. It should remain consistently moist but not waterlogged.

6. Thin seedlings.

   As seedlings emerge and grow, you may need to thin them to the recommended spacing specified on the seed packets. Crowded seedlings can compete for resources, leading to stunted growth and decreased productivity. Gently remove excess seedlings to provide ample room for healthy development.

By following these germination tips and understanding how to sow seeds directly in garden soil, you'll be well-prepared for a successful start to your gardening season, whether you're nurturing seedlings indoors or sowing seeds directly in your garden beds.

Transplanting Young Seedlings

Once your seeds have germinated and sprouted into beautiful healthy seedlings, it's time to transplant them.

Step 1: Prepare Your Transplanting Area

1. Before you begin transplanting, make sure the garden bed or larger containers are ready. This means they should be free of weeds and debris, providing a clean environment for your seedlings.

2. Water the soil in the transplanting area thoroughly the day before or the morning of transplanting. Soil that is evenly moist will make it easier for the seedlings to adapt to their new location.

Step 2: Timing and Inspection

Timing is crucial for successful transplanting. Ensure that your seedlings are at the right stage for transplanting.

1. Typically, seedlings should have at least two sets of true leaves. True leaves are the second set of leaves that appear after the initial seedling leaves (cotyledons). The seedlings should also be about 2-3 inches (5-7.5 cm) tall.

2. Inspect the seedlings carefully for any signs of pests, diseases, or other issues. Address any problems before transplanting to prevent them from spreading to healthy seedlings.

Step 3: Preparing Seedlings for Transplant

1. Water the seedlings in their original containers before transplanting. This ensures that the root ball is well-hydrated and helps keep it intact during the transplanting process.

2. To remove the seedlings, gently squeeze the sides of the container or use a tool like a dibber to loosen the soil around the root ball.

3. Carefully lift the seedlings out while holding them by their leaves or the root ball, avoiding any damage to the stems.

Step 4: Transplanting Seedlings

1. Dig a hole in the transplanting area that is approximately the same size as the root ball of the seedling. You can use a trowel or your fingers to create the hole.

2. Carefully place the seedling in the hole at the same depth it was growing in its original container.

3. Planting at the correct depth ensures that the seedling's roots are properly situated in the soil.

4. Space the seedlings according to the recommended spacing for the specific plant species. Proper spacing ensures that the plants have enough room to grow without competing with each other.

Step 5: Protect Seedlings From Weather and Water

If you're transplanting on a windy or sunny day, provide temporary protection for the seedlings. You can use items like shade cloth, overturned pots, or fabric row covers to shield them from harsh conditions.

Water the transplanted seedlings immediately after planting. This helps settle the soil around the roots and provides the seedlings with immediate hydration.

Step 6: Mulch and Maintain Consistent Moisture

After transplanting, apply a layer of organic mulch, such as straw or shredded leaves, around the base of the seedlings. Mulch helps conserve soil moisture, suppresses weed growth, and regulates soil temperature.

Keep the soil consistently moist during the first few weeks after transplanting. Adequate moisture helps the seedlings establish their roots in their new environment. Water deeply when needed but avoid waterlogging the soil.

Step 7: Monitor and Support Growth

1. Continuously monitor the transplanted seedlings for any signs of stress, pests, or diseases. Early detection allows for timely intervention.

2. Provide any necessary support as the seedlings grow. For taller plants, use stakes or supports to prevent bending or breaking. Implement pest control measures as needed to protect the seedlings.

These steps will help you have a smooth and successful transition for your young seedlings as they adapt to their new growing environment. Keep in mind that proper care and attention during transplanting are essential for their healthy development.

CHAPTER 6:

Watering Techniques and Irrigation

O ur botanical companions, diverse in form and temperament, each have unique thirsts that call for your attention. In this section, we embark on a voyage to unravel the profound mysteries of catering to various plant species.

In this chapter, we dive into the art and science of watering your garden, recognizing that every plant has its own unique thirst that requires your attention. Understanding the language of plants and their individual hydration requirements is fundamental to successful gardening.

Let's explore the factors that influence how much water each plant species truly craves.

Understanding the Watering Needs of Different Plants

To ensure the health and vitality of your plants, it's essential to understand their specific watering requirements. Different plants have varying needs when it comes to water, and providing the right amount at the right time is crucial. It ensures that each plant receives the appropriate amount of water at the right time.

In order to make sure your plants receive the right amount of water, it is important to research the selection of plants that you plan on growing. Look into the native habitat of the plants and the level of drought tolerance they have.

1. Native habitat

   Research the natural habitat of the plants you intend to grow. Understanding where they originate from can provide valuable insights into their water requirements. For example, plants native to arid regions are likely more drought-tolerant.

2. Drought tolerance

   Consider the drought tolerance of your chosen plants. Some species are naturally adapted to thrive in dry conditions and require less frequent watering, while others may need more consistent moisture.

Also, look into the watering preferences of each type of plant.

Water Preferences

Different plants have varying preferences when it comes to soil moisture levels. Some prefer well-drained soil, while others thrive in consistently moist conditions. Make sure your garden's soil type aligns with the preferences of your selected plants.

Here's a general guide you can follow when it comes to watering your plants:

Vegetables and Annuals
- Vegetables and annuals typically require consistent moisture to thrive.

- Water deeply, providing about 1 to 1.5 inches (2.5 to 3.8 cm) of water per week, either through rainfall or irrigation.

- Focus on watering the root zone to encourage healthy root development and prevent diseases by keeping foliage dry.

Perennials
- Perennials often have varying water needs based on their specific species and growing conditions.

- As a general rule, water perennials deeply when the top inch (2.5 cm) of soil feels dry to the touch.

- Established perennials may require less frequent watering than newly planted ones.

Shrubs
- Shrubs can have diverse water requirements based on their species and size.

- Newly planted shrubs need more frequent watering until they become established, typically in the first year.

- Water deeply to encourage deep root growth, which makes shrubs more drought-resistant.

Trees

- Trees vary widely in their water needs, with factors like species, age, and size playing a role.

- Newly planted trees require regular watering to establish their root systems. Provide deep, slow watering.

- Mature trees generally require less frequent watering but benefit from deep watering during prolonged dry spells.

Houseplants

- Houseplants have different water requirements, with factors like the type of plant, pot size, and indoor conditions affecting their needs.

- Water houseplants when the top inch (2.5 cm) of soil feels dry. Be cautious not to overwater, as root rot can be a common issue with indoor plants.

Succulents and Cacti

- Succulents and cacti are adapted to arid conditions and prefer infrequent, deep watering.

- Allow the soil to dry out completely between waterings, and water sparingly during their dormant periods, typically in winter.

Native and Drought-Tolerant Plants

- Native and drought-tolerant plants are adapted to local conditions and often require less water.

- Water these plants sparingly, allowing the soil to dry slightly between waterings. They may thrive on rainfall alone once established.

Groundcovers and Lawns

Groundcovers and lawns have specific water needs.

- Lawns may require about 1 to 1.5 inches (2.5 to 3.8 cm) of water per week during the growing season.

- Water deeply and infrequently to encourage deep root growth.

- Groundcovers vary, so consult plant-specific guidelines for optimal watering.

Keep in mind when growing different types of plants together, such as vegetables and flowers, that they need to have the same watering requirements. Group plants with similar water requirements together in your garden. This practice, known as hydrozoning, allows you to create watering zones that cater to the specific needs of different plant groups. It promotes efficient water usage and prevents overwatering or underwatering.

The amount of water different types of plants need can vary significantly depending on several factors, including the plant species, local climate, soil type, and stage of growth.

Let's delve deeper into how to adjust your watering practices for plants at different growth stages and in various weather conditions.

Seedlings and Young Plants

Watering Frequency

- Seedlings and young plants have underdeveloped root systems so they rely on frequent, shallow watering.

- Keep the soil consistently moist but avoid waterlogged conditions.

- Water seedlings gently to prevent soil disturbance.

Amount

- Water with care to prevent dislodging or damaging delicate seedlings.

- Use a fine spray or a mist setting on your watering can or hose nozzle.

- Water enough to moisten the top inch (2.5 cm) of soil.

Weather Conditions

- In hot, dry weather, seedlings may require daily or twice-daily watering.

- Use shade cloth or other means to protect young plants from excessive sun and wind.

Established Plants (Adult Growth)
Watering Frequency

- Established plants generally require less frequent watering because they have deeper root systems.

- Water when the top 2-3 inches (5-7.5 cm) of soil feels dry to the touch.

Amount

- Water deeply to encourage deep root growth.

- Provide enough water to penetrate the root zone, typically 6-8 inches (15-20 cm) deep.

Weather Conditions

- During hot, dry spells, mature plants may need more frequent watering.

- In cooler or rainy periods, reduce watering to prevent overhydration.

Flowering and Fruiting Stage
Watering Frequency

- Plants in the flowering and fruiting stage often have increased water needs to support the development of flowers and fruits.

- Keep the soil consistently moist as fluctuations in soil moisture can lead to blossom drop or fruit cracking.

Amount

- Continue deep watering to ensure the root system can access the necessary moisture.

- Apply enough water to maintain even soil moisture around the plant.

Weather Conditions

- During hot, dry weather, pay special attention to watering flowering and fruiting plants to prevent stress that can affect fruit quality.

Extreme Heat and Drought Conditions

Watering Frequency

- During heatwaves and droughts, all plants may require more frequent watering.

- Monitor soil moisture daily and water as needed to prevent wilting.

Amount

- Increase the amount of water applied to ensure moisture reaches deep into the soil where the roots can access it.

- Consider watering early in the morning or late in the evening to minimize water loss through evaporation.

Water Conservation

- Mulching is especially important during extreme heat and drought to reduce soil moisture evaporation and conserve water.

Rainy Periods
Watering Frequency

- During rainy periods, assess soil moisture regularly.

- Reduce or suspend watering if the soil becomes saturated to avoid waterlogging and root rot.

Amount

- Adjust the amount of water based on the amount of rainfall. You may not need to water at all if there is sufficient natural precipitation.

Cold and Winter Months
Watering Frequency

- In colder months, plants generally require less water as their growth slows.

- Reduce the frequency of watering, but don't let the soil completely dry out.

Amount

- Apply enough water to maintain some moisture in the soil to sustain the plant's root system through winter.

- Be cautious not to overwater during cold weather as this can lead to root rot.

By following these guidelines and closely observing your plants and their specific needs, you can fine-tune your watering practices to ensure optimal growth and health under various growth stages and weather conditions. Remember that the key is to provide the right amount of water when it's needed to prevent both underwatering and overwatering.

Observation

Regularly inspect your plants for any signs of water stress; these could be signs such as

- wilting leaves
  - Wilting leaves that don't recover in the evening can be a sign of insufficient water.

- yellowing or browning foliage
  - Yellowing or browning of leaves can occur due to both overwatering (root rot) and underwatering (lack of nutrients reaching the roots).

- decreased growth
  - Stunted growth or a noticeable lack of new growth can indicate water-related issues.

Temporary vs. Prolonged Wilting

There is a difference between temporary wilting and prolonged wilting. Temporary wilting can occur during hot periods of the day but as the night rolls in and everything cools down plants will recover. Watering during temporary wilting is usually unnecessary and can lead to overwatering. Prolonged wilting, on the other hand, suggests a genuine need for water.

Soil Moisture Testing

Apart from watching your plants for physical signs that they might need water (which is often a little late), there are two main moisture tests you can do.

Moisture Meter

A moisture meter is a handy tool that measures the moisture content of the soil. Insert the probe into the soil near the plant's root zone to determine whether it's time to water. Most moisture meters come with instructions, and they give you readings on a scale from dry to wet.

Finger Test

Stick your finger about an inch into the soil. If the soil feels dry at that depth, it's typically a good indicator that it's time to water. However, this method may not be as precise as using a moisture meter, but it does work.

Watering Techniques

A very good question all beginner gardeners ask, and you might also be wondering about this, is when to water and if there are any best techniques.

Base Watering

When watering, target the base of the plant and aim for the root zone. This ensures that water is delivered directly to the roots where it's needed most. Avoid overhead watering, especially in the evening, as wet foliage overnight can promote fungal diseases.

Timing

Water early in the morning or late in the evening to reduce water loss through evaporation. Morning watering allows the plant to take up moisture before the heat of the day, while evening watering helps replenish soil moisture levels overnight.

By conducting thorough research, closely observing your plants, and employing appropriate watering techniques, you can meet the specific water needs of each plant in your garden, fostering their health and vitality while conserving water and preventing common issues like overwatering and underwatering.

It's essential to monitor your plants and adapt your watering schedule based on their specific needs. Factors like soil type, weather conditions, and the presence of mulch can also influence watering requirements. Pay attention to signs of overwatering (wilting or yellowing leaves) and underwatering (wilting or dry soil), and adjust your watering accordingly to maintain healthy plants. Remember that watering needs can change with the seasons, so be flexible with your watering schedule.

Efficient Irrigation Systems

Apart from a regular watering can and hose, there is a huge variety of different irrigation systems you can make use of. Let's look at some of the popular methods, how they work, and a general guide on how to install them.

Drip Irrigation

Precise Watering

Drip irrigation's precision is highly beneficial for plant health. It delivers water directly to the root zone, where plants need it most, reducing the risk of overwatering or underwatering.

Precise watering helps prevent water wastage by ensuring that water is used efficiently by the plants, promoting optimal growth.

Customizable Emitters

The ability to customize emitters with different flow rates is a powerful feature. It allows you to tailor the irrigation system to the specific water needs of various plant species and even individual plants.

For example, you can provide more water to thirsty plants like tomatoes while giving drought-tolerant plants like succulents just the right amount.

Conservation of Water

Drip irrigation is a water-efficient method that minimizes runoff and evaporation, making it an excellent choice for sustainable gardening.

By conserving water resources, you contribute to environmental sustainability and reduce water bills, particularly in areas with water scarcity or restrictions.

Weed Control

Drip irrigation's targeted water delivery significantly reduces moisture in the surrounding soil, making it less conducive to weed growth.

This weed control benefit not only saves time and effort but also minimizes competition for water and nutrients among garden plants.

How to install a Drip Irrigation System

Installing a drip irrigation system is a great way to efficiently water your garden. Here's a step-by-step guide on how to install a basic drip irrigation system:

Materials you'll need

1. Drip irrigation kit (includes tubing, emitters, connectors, stakes, and filter)

2. Garden hose or water source

3. Pressure regulator (if not included in the kit)

4. Hole punch tool or small drill

5. Scissors or pipe cutter

6. Timer (optional, for automated watering)

7. Mulch (optional)

8. Shovel or trowel (for burying tubing, if preferred)

Step-by-Step installation

1. Plan your system.

    o Determine the layout of your garden beds and the location of your plants.

    o Decide where you'll place the main water supply line and where you want to position the emitters for each plant.

    o Ensure that you have a nearby water source, such as a garden hose connection.

2. Prepare the main water supply line.

    o Attach the pressure regulator to the garden hose or water source to reduce the water pressure to an appropriate level for your irrigation system.

    o Connect the filter (if included in your kit) to the pressure regulator.

    o Attach the tubing to the filter.

3. Lay out the tubing.

    o Unroll the tubing along the paths where you want to position the irrigation lines.

- Secure the tubing in place using stakes or landscape pins. Make sure it's elevated slightly to allow for proper water flow.

4. Cut and insert emitters.

- Cut the tubing where you want to place emitters for individual plants.

- Use a hole punch tool or a small drill to make holes in the tubing at the desired locations.

- Insert emitters into the holes you've created. Make sure they are securely attached.

5. Connect tubing sections.

- Use the connectors provided in your kit to join tubing sections. You may need T-connectors, elbow connectors, or straight connectors, depending on your layout.

6. Test the system.

- Turn on the water source to test your irrigation system. Check for leaks or any issues with water flow.

- Adjust the flow rate of the emitters if needed to ensure proper watering for each plant.

7. Bury the Tubing (optional).

   o You can bury the tubing to conceal it and protect it from damage. Use a shovel or trowel to create a shallow trench and bury the tubing while leaving the emitters exposed.

8. Install a timer (optional).

   o If you want automated watering, install a timer on the hose or water source. Set the timer according to your garden's watering needs.

9. Mulch (optional).

   o Apply mulch, such as wood chips or straw, around your plants to help retain soil moisture and reduce evaporation.

   o Mulch also protects the tubing from UV damage.

10. Perform regular maintenance.

   o Periodically check your system for clogs, leaks, or damaged components.

   o Adjust your watering schedule as needed based on seasonal changes and plant growth.

Remember that this is a basic guide for installing a drip irrigation system. More complex systems may involve additional components like valves, multiple zones, and a backflow preventer for larger gardens or lawns. Always follow the manufacturer's instructions provided with your irrigation kit, and consider consulting a professional if you're dealing with a complex installation or have specific requirements.

Soaker Hoses

Slow, Even Watering

Soaker hoses are designed to provide slow and consistent watering by allowing water to seep out gradually along their entire length.

This gradual release ensures that water penetrates deeply into the soil, promoting healthier root development and reducing the risk of shallow surface roots.

Flexible Layout

Soaker hoses are versatile and adaptable to various garden layouts. You have the flexibility to lay them along the base of plants, arrange them in zigzag patterns through garden beds, or even bury them beneath mulch.

This adaptability allows you to efficiently water different plant arrangements, making them suitable for both flower beds and vegetable gardens.

Water Conservation

Similar to drip irrigation, soaker hoses excel in water conservation by minimizing runoff and evaporation.

Consistent soil moisture is maintained, which is especially beneficial for plant health and growth. Less water is wasted, and you can maximize the use of available water resources.

How to Install a Soaker Hose System

Installing soaker hoses is a straightforward process and can be an effective way to provide slow, even watering to your garden beds, flower beds, or vegetable gardens. Here's a step-by-step guide on how to install soaker hoses:

Materials you'll need

1. Soaker hoses (appropriate length for your garden area)

2. Hose fittings (end caps and connectors)

3. Garden hose (if needed)

4. Hose stakes or garden staples

5. Timer (optional, for automated watering)

6. Mulch (optional)

Step-by-step installation

1. Plan your layout.

    o Determine the layout of your garden beds and where you want to position the soaker hoses.

    o Consider the placement of plants and the spacing of the hoses to ensure even coverage.

    o Measure the total length of soaker hose you'll need for your garden beds.

2. Attach end caps and connectors.

   o If necessary, cut the soaker hose to the desired length using scissors or a sharp knife.

   o Attach an end cap to one end of the soaker hose to seal it. If your garden requires multiple hoses, connect them using hose connectors.

   o Ensure a secure fit.

3. Connect to a water source.

   o You have two options here:

      ■ Direct connection: Attach the soaker hose directly to an outdoor faucet using a garden hose if the faucet is near your garden. Use a hose splitter if you want to connect multiple hoses.

      ■ Use a garden hose: If your water source is farther from the garden, connect a garden hose to the faucet and then attach the soaker hose to the garden hose.

4. Lay out the soaker hoses.

   o Lay the soaker hoses along the base of your plants or garden beds. Position them in a serpentine or zigzag pattern to ensure even watering.

- o Keep the hoses slightly elevated above the soil surface to prevent clogging and allow for better water distribution.

5. Secure the hoses.

- o Use hose stakes, garden staples, or U-shaped pins to secure the soaker hoses in place. This prevents them from shifting and ensures consistent coverage.

- o Place stakes or staples every 1-2 feet (30-60 cm) along the length of the hose.

6. Test the system.

- o Turn on the water source and allow the soaker hoses to run for a few minutes to ensure they are functioning correctly. Check for any leaks or irregularities.

7. Adjust the water flow.

- o You can regulate the water flow by adjusting the water pressure at the source or by using a flow control valve if your soaker hose kit includes one.

8. Install a timer (optional).

- o For automated watering, you can attach a timer to the faucet or hose to control when the soaker hoses operate. Set the timer according to your garden's watering needs.

9. Mulch (optional).

    ○ Apply mulch, such as wood chips or straw, around your plants and over the soaker hoses. Mulch helps retain soil moisture, reduces evaporation, and prevents damage to the hoses from UV rays.

10. Perform regular maintenance.

    ○ Periodically inspect your soaker hoses for clogs, leaks, or damage. Clear any clogs and replace damaged sections as needed.

    ○ Adjust the watering schedule based on seasonal changes and plant growth.

Soaker hoses provide slow, consistent moisture to your garden, promoting deep root growth and efficient water use. Proper installation and maintenance will help ensure the health and vitality of your plants while conserving water.

Smart Irrigation Controllers

Data-Driven Watering

Smart controllers use data from weather forecasts, soil moisture sensors, and plant type information to create customized watering schedules for your garden.

This data-driven approach ensures that your plants receive the precise amount of water they need, reducing the risk of both under and overwatering. It promotes healthier plants and conserves water resources.

Remote Control

The ability to manage your irrigation system remotely via smartphone apps or web interfaces provides unmatched convenience and flexibility.

Whether you're at home or away, you can monitor and adjust your system on the go, ensuring that your garden's water requirements are met effectively.

Efficient Water Management

Smart controllers go beyond fixed schedules. They adapt to real-time weather conditions, automatically adjusting watering times and duration based on factors like temperature, humidity, and rainfall.

This level of efficiency not only conserves water but also helps prevent overwatering, reducing the risk of plant stress, disease, and water wastage.

How to Install a Smart Irrigation Controller

Installing a smart irrigation controller allows you to efficiently manage your garden's watering schedule based on real-time weather conditions and plant needs. Here's a step-by-step guide on how to install a smart irrigation controller.

Materials you'll need

1. Smart irrigation controller

2. Smartphone or tablet with a compatible app (for setup and control)

3. Wi-Fi network and internet access

4. Screwdriver

5. Optional: Mounting hardware (screws and anchors), drill, and level

Step-by-step installation

1. Select a suitable location.

    o   Choose a location for your smart irrigation controller near your outdoor water source and within the Wi-Fi range. This is typically near your existing irrigation system, such as a valve manifold.

    o   Ensure the controller is protected from direct sunlight and exposure to extreme weather conditions.

2. Turn off the water supply.

    o   Turn off the main water supply to your irrigation system to ensure there's no water pressure while installing the controller.

3. Remove the old controller (if applicable).

    o   If you're replacing an existing irrigation controller, disconnect and remove the old controller from the wall or mounting location.

4. Install the smart controller.

   ○ Mount the smart irrigation controller on the wall using the provided mounting hardware, if needed. Use a level to ensure it's straight.

   ○ If you're replacing an old controller, connect the existing wires to the corresponding zones on the new controller. Label the wires if necessary.

   ○ If it's a new installation, you'll need to connect wires from your irrigation valves to the controller's zone terminals. Refer to the controller's user manual for guidance on wiring.

5. Connect to power.

   ○ Plug the controller into a nearby electrical outlet. Make sure it's a GFCI-protected outlet for safety.

   ○ If your controller is battery-powered or solar-powered, follow the manufacturer's instructions for power setup.

6. Connect to Wi-Fi.

   ○ Power on the smart controller and follow the manufacturer's instructions to connect it to your Wi-Fi network using the compatible smartphone or tablet app.

- This typically involves scanning a QR code, selecting your Wi-Fi network, and entering the network password.

7. Set up the controller.

    - Open the app on your smartphone or tablet and follow the on-screen prompts to set up the controller.

    - Configure your irrigation zones, plant types, and watering schedules based on your garden's needs and local weather conditions.

8. Test the system.

    - After setup, perform a test run to ensure the controller is functioning correctly.

    - Run each zone manually and verify that water is being delivered to the desired areas.

    - Check for any leaks, irregularities, or issues with water flow.

9. Schedule and monitor.

    - Customize your watering schedule and frequency through the app. You can often set specific days and times for each zone.

○ Take advantage of the smart features, such as weather data integration, to allow the controller to adjust watering based on local weather conditions.

10. Perform regular maintenance.

○ Periodically check the controller's app for updates or firmware upgrades to ensure optimal performance.

○ Monitor your garden's watering needs and adjust the schedule as needed to accommodate seasonal changes and plant growth.

Once your smart irrigation controller is installed and configured, it will provide efficient and automated control over your garden's irrigation, helping you conserve water and maintain healthy plants.

By incorporating these efficient irrigation systems and practices into your gardening routine, you can promote healthy plant growth, reduce water waste, and contribute to a more sustainable and thriving garden.

Rain Barrels and Rainwater Harvesting

Rain barrels and rainwater harvesting provide an eco-friendly and cost-effective way to collect and store rainwater for various uses, including garden irrigation.

Rain barrels are large containers designed to collect and store rainwater that runs off your roof during rain events. Rainwater harvesting, which involves capturing and storing rainwater for later use, is an eco-friendly practice that offers several benefits:

1. Eco-friendly water source

   Rain barrels allow you to collect and store rainwater, reducing your reliance on treated municipal water. This conserves water resources and lowers your water bills.

   Using rainwater for irrigation and other outdoor purposes reduces the demand for potable water, which is treated to drinking water standards. This, in turn, reduces the energy and chemicals needed for water treatment.

2. Supplemental irrigation

   The collected rainwater can be used to supplement your garden's irrigation needs during dry spells, droughts, or water restrictions.

   Rainwater is naturally soft and free from chlorine and other chemicals commonly found in tap water. It can benefit many types of plants by providing them with water that is closer to their natural environment.

3. Reduce stormwater runoff

   Rain barrels help reduce stormwater runoff, which can contribute to soil erosion and water pollution by carrying pollutants into waterways.

By capturing rainwater from your roof, you play a part in reducing the volume of runoff, potentially benefiting the local environment.

How to Harvest and Store Rainwater

1. Collecting surface

    o Install gutters and downspouts on your roof if you don't already have them.

    o These will direct rainwater into your collection system.

    o Ensure your gutters and downspouts are clean and free from debris to prevent clogs.

2. Selecting rain barrels

    o Choose one or more rain barrels with a combined capacity that suits your needs.

    o You can purchase rain barrels at garden centers or home improvement stores.

    o Consider whether you want an open or closed system, with or without a screen or filter to prevent debris from entering the barrel.

3. Installing the rain barrel

    o Place the rain barrel on a stable, level surface, such as a concrete pad or cinder blocks.

    o Elevating the barrel allows you to easily access the spigot by attaching a hose or filling watering cans.

4. Connecting the downspout

   o Position the rain barrel beneath a downspout that diverts water from your roof.

   o Cut the downspout where it will connect to the barrel using a hacksaw or tin snips.

   o Attach a diverter kit to the downspout and direct the flow into the rain barrel. Some kits include a filter to remove debris.

5. Plumbing connections

   o Install an overflow hose or pipe near the top of the barrel to direct excess water away from the foundation.

   o Add a spigot near the bottom of the barrel to access the stored rainwater. You can attach a hose or fill containers directly from the spigot.

6. Maintenance

   o Regularly inspect the rain barrel for debris and clean the screen or filter to ensure water flows freely.

   o Empty and disconnect the barrel before freezing temperatures to prevent damage.

7. Usage

   o Use the collected rainwater for garden irrigation, watering plants, and other outdoor purposes.

- ○ Monitor the water level in the barrel and adjust your usage based on your garden's needs and rainfall patterns.

By harvesting, storing, and utilizing rainwater, you can promote sustainability, reduce your environmental impact, and save money on water bills while nurturing your garden with natural, chemical-free water.

Regular inspections of your irrigation system are essential for identifying leaks, clogs, or damaged components. Addressing these issues promptly not only prevents water wastage but also ensures the continued efficiency of your system.

Adjusting your watering schedule based on seasonal changes is vital. Plants have varying water requirements throughout the year, with increased needs during hot summer months and reduced needs during cooler, wetter periods. Adapting your irrigation schedule accordingly ensures optimal plant health.

Organic mulch, like wood chips or straw, acts as a barrier that reduces soil moisture evaporation. It keeps the soil consistently moist, reducing the frequency of watering while promoting plant health. Mulch also serves as a natural weed barrier, minimizing weed growth. This decreases competition for water and nutrients, benefiting your garden plants.

Mulch helps regulate soil temperature by insulating it. It keeps the soil cooler during hot weather and provides some insulation during colder seasons, which can be beneficial for plant root systems.

By combining a deep understanding of your plant's water requirements with efficient irrigation methods and smart watering practices, you can create an effective and sustainable watering strategy for your garden. This approach will not only promote plant health but also conserve water and reduce the time and effort you spend on watering.

CHAPTER 7:
Nurturing Your Plants

A fter you've planned, planted, and have your water technique down to a T, your garden is thriving. But what to do now? That is the beauty of gardening; there is always something to do, such as a new project to take on, the completion of an exciting project, edibles to harvest, or just simply observing your garden—and keeping your plants healthy and protecting them from pests and diseases.

Let's explore some of the essential techniques for nurturing your plants, including pruning and thinning for optimal growth and protecting your garden from pests and diseases.

Pruning and Thinning for Optimal Growth

Pruning and thinning are essential practices to shape, manage, and maintain the health of certain types of plants.

Pruning is the process of selectively removing parts of a plant, such as branches, leaves, flowers, or fruit, to achieve specific objectives. It is a common practice used for various purposes such as:

- promoting plant health
  - Pruning can remove diseased, dead, or damaged plant parts, preventing the spread of diseases and improving overall plant health.

- shaping and training
  - Pruning is often used to shape plants and encourage them to grow in a particular form or structure.
  - For example, shaping fruit trees or topiaries.

- enhancing aesthetic appeal
  - Pruning can improve the appearance of a plant by removing overgrown or unsightly branches, making it more visually pleasing.

- boosting fruit production
  - In fruit-bearing plants, pruning can increase the quality and quantity of fruit by removing excess branches or thinning fruit clusters.

- managing size
  - Pruning can control the size of a plant, preventing it from becoming too large or encroaching on nearby structures or pathways.

- improving air circulation and sunlight exposure
  - Proper pruning can open up the canopy of a plant, allowing for better air circulation and increased sunlight penetration.
  - This reduces the risk of fungal diseases and promotes photosynthesis.

Pruning methods and timing vary depending on the type of plant, its growth habits, and the specific objectives.

Thinning can be seen as the same as pruning, but thinning is done more selectively with specific objectives in mind, such as removing parts of a plant to reduce overcrowding and improve the overall spacing between branches, leaves, or fruit. The primary goal of thinning is to ensure that the remaining plant parts receive adequate resources and, as a result, grow more vigorously.

While pruning is something we do at certain times, like at the end or beginning of seasons, thinning is done at any time as needed. We thin certain plants in order to

- enhance air circulation.
  - Thinning out dense foliage or fruit clusters improves air circulation within the plant, reducing humidity and the risk of fungal diseases.

- increase sunlight exposure.

  - By removing excess leaves or fruit, thinning allows more sunlight to reach the remaining plant parts, which is essential for photosynthesis and fruit ripening.

- prevent overcrowding.

  - Thinning prevents plants from becoming overcrowded, which can lead to competition for nutrients and light and hinder healthy growth.

- improve fruit quality.

  - In fruit-bearing plants, thinning fruit clusters ensure that the remaining fruit receives enough nutrients and space to develop to its full potential, resulting in larger, tastier fruit.

Thinning methods and timing depend on the type of plant and the desired spacing between branches or fruit. It is often done by hand, where excess plant parts are carefully pruned or pinched off. Thinning can also be used to manage the population of pests, like removing unwanted or invasive seedlings from a garden bed.

Pruning and thinning are essential techniques for managing plant growth, maintaining plant health, and optimizing crop yields in gardens and orchards.

Let's look at some examples of plants that can be pruned and thinned and that benefit greatly from it.

Vegetables That Respond to Pruning and Thinning

Below you will find a general list of common plants you will encounter and how to prune or thin them.

Tools you will need include

- hand pruners
- loppers
- pruning saws
- shears

Tomatoes

Pruning tomatoes involves removing the "suckers," which are small shoots that form in the leaf axils (the space between the stem and a leaf).

When to prune tomatoes: Prune when the suckers are small and easily pinched off, typically when they are about 2-4 inches long.

How to prune tomatoes: Pinch off the suckers using your fingers or pruning shears, being careful not to damage the main stem. Aim to maintain one or two main stems for determinate varieties and 1-2 main stems for indeterminate varieties.

Peppers

Peppers benefit from thinning by removing some of the smaller fruit, allowing the plant to channel its energy into growing larger and tastier fruit.

When to thin peppers: Thin peppers when they are still small and immature, ideally when they are about the size of a golf ball.

How to thin peppers: Gently pluck or cut the smaller fruit from the plant, leaving a sufficient gap between the remaining peppers to allow for healthy growth.

Cucumbers

Pruning cucumber vines involves removing excessive foliage and lateral branches to improve air circulation and reduce the risk of powdery mildew.

When to prune cucumbers: Begin pruning cucumbers once they have developed several sets of true leaves, and the vines start to sprawl.

How to prune cucumbers: Use pruning shears or scissors to snip away excess foliage and lateral branches, keeping the main stem and necessary leaves intact.

Fruit Trees

Pruning fruit trees is essential for shaping the tree, managing its size, and ensuring sunlight penetrates the canopy.

When to prune fruit trees: Prune during the dormant season, typically in late winter or early spring before new growth begins. This reduces the risk of disease transmission and minimizes stress on the tree.

How to prune fruit trees: Pruning techniques vary depending on the type of fruit tree and desired shape. Consult pruning guides specific to your tree variety for detailed instructions.

Grapevines

Pruning grapevines promotes proper air circulation, encourages fruit production, and helps maintain the desired shape of the vine.

When to prune: Grapevines are typically pruned during late winter or early spring when they are dormant, before new growth begins.

How to prune: Remove dead or diseased wood as well as excess growth from the previous season. Depending on the type of grapevine and desired structure, pruning methods can vary.

Roses

Pruning roses helps rejuvenate the plant, encourages new growth, removes dead or diseased wood, and promotes better flowering.

When to prune: The timing depends on the type of rose, but generally, pruning is done in late winter or early spring, just before new growth emerges.

How to prune: Remove dead or damaged canes, thin out crowded growth, and shape the plant as desired. Different types of roses (e.g., hybrid teas, and shrub roses) may require specific pruning techniques.

Blueberry Bushes

Pruning blueberry bushes enhances fruit production, maintains plant health, and prevents overcrowding.

When to prune: Prune blueberry bushes during late winter or early spring before bud break.

How to prune: Remove dead, weak, or low-hanging branches. Thin out crowded growth and cut back older canes to encourage new growth and better fruiting.

Peach Trees

Pruning peach trees helps maintain their shape, increases sunlight exposure to fruit, and reduces disease risk.

When to prune: Prune peach trees during late winter or early spring, while they are still dormant.

How to prune: Remove dead, diseased, or crossing branches. Open up the center of the tree to improve air circulation. Peach trees are often pruned to have an open, vase-like structure.

Berry Bushes (e.g., Raspberry and Blackberry)

Pruning berry bushes promotes better fruit production, removes old canes, and manages their growth.

When to prune: Prune raspberry and blackberry bushes during late winter or early spring before new growth starts.

How to prune: Remove spent canes that have borne fruit, leaving behind healthy, new canes for the next season. Thin out crowded growth and prune back excessively long canes to encourage branching.

Note: Proper pruning and thinning tailored to each plant type contributes to healthier plants, larger yields, and reduced susceptibility to diseases and pests. Always refer to specific guidelines for each plant variety as pruning methods may vary.

By following the appropriate pruning and thinning practices for your plants and timing these tasks correctly, you can maximize their health and yield while minimizing the risk of disease and overcrowding. Proper care and attention to your garden's needs will result in a more productive and thriving garden.

Protecting Your Garden From Pests and Diseases

Protecting your garden from pests and diseases is crucial to ensuring the health and productivity of your plants.

Let's first have a look at different pests that you might encounter, how to identify them, and how to deal with them in an organic way.

Pests

Aphids

Appearance: Tiny, soft-bodied insects often found in clusters on plant stems and leaves.

Organic Control:

- Use a strong stream of water to dislodge aphids from plants.

- Attract natural predators like ladybugs, lacewings, and parasitic wasps.

- Spray plants with neem oil or insecticidal soap.

Whiteflies

Appearance: Small, white, moth-like insects with a powdery appearance when disturbed.

Organic Control:

- Release ladybugs and lacewings.
- Apply neem oil or insecticidal soap.
- Yellow sticky traps can help catch adult whiteflies.

Caterpillars

Appearance: Soft-bodied larvae that vary in color and may have distinct markings. They can be found eating leaves and often curl into a C-shape when disturbed.

Organic Control:

- Handpick caterpillars and eggs.
- Attract parasitic wasps and predatory insects like lacewings.
- Apply Bacillus thuringiensis (Bt), a natural bacterium that kills caterpillars but is safe for other insects.

Slugs and Snails

Appearance: Soft-bodied, slimy creatures with coiled shells (snails) or without (slugs).

Organic Control:

- Place copper tape around plant beds.
- Set up beer traps.
- Handpick slugs and snails during the nighttime.
- Apply diatomaceous earth around plants.

Spider Mites

Appearance: Tiny, often red or yellow insects that leave fine webs on plants. They are usually found on the underside of leaves.

Organic Control:

- Spray plants with a strong stream of water to wash off mites.
- Introduce predatory mites, such as Phytoseiulus persimilis.
- Apply neem oil or insecticidal soap.

Japanese Beetles

Appearance: Shiny, metallic green beetles with copper-colored wings.

Organic Control:

- Handpick beetles early in the morning when they are less active.
- Apply neem oil or pyrethrin-based insecticides.

Thrips

Appearance: Tiny, slender insects that may be yellow, black, or brown.

Organic Control:

- Use yellow sticky traps to monitor and trap thrips.
- Spray plants with insecticidal soap or neem oil.

Scale Insects

Appearance: Tiny, immobile insects often covered with protective waxy scales that resemble small bumps on stems and leaves.

Organic Control:

- Scrape off scales with a soft brush or cloth.
- Apply neem oil or horticultural oil during the dormant season when scales are most vulnerable.

Mealybugs

Appearance: Small, soft-bodied insects covered in a white, cottony substance.

Organic Control:

- Remove mealybugs with a cotton swab soaked in rubbing alcohol.
- Spray plants with neem oil or insecticidal soap.

Flea Beetles

Appearance: Small, jumping insects that may be black or brown.

Organic Control:

- Use row covers to protect young plants.
- Plant trap crops like radishes to attract flea beetles away from valuable crops.
- Apply diatomaceous earth around plants.

Earwigs

Appearance: Long, flattened insects with pincers on their rear end.

Organic Control:

- Provide hiding places like rolled newspaper traps.
- Set up shallow dishes of vegetable oil as traps.
- Remove debris and weeds where earwigs hide.

Cutworms

Appearance: Soft-bodied caterpillars that are typically gray, brown, or black.

Organic Control:

- Use collars made of cardboard or aluminum foil around young plants to prevent cutworms from attacking stems.
- Handpick cutworms during nighttime patrols.

Leafhoppers
Appearance: Small, wedge-shaped insects often green or brown in color.

Organic Control:

- Attract beneficial insects like ladybugs and lacewings.
- Spray plants with neem oil or insecticidal soap.

Squash Bugs
Appearance: Shield-shaped insects that are typically brown or gray with orange or red markings.

Organic Control:

- Handpick and destroy squash bugs and eggs.
- Use row covers to protect plants.
- Companion plant with nasturtiums to deter squash bugs.

Rodents (e.g., Rats, Mice, Voles)
Appearance: Various, but often small mammals with fur and long tails.

Organic Control:

- Set up snap traps or live traps.
- Use natural repellents like peppermint oil or garlic sprays.
- Keep garden areas clean and remove potential nesting sites.

Deer

Appearance: Medium to large mammals with fur and distinctive hooves.

Organic Control:

- Use deer-resistant plants.
- Install deer fencing or netting.
- Apply deer-repellent sprays with natural ingredients like hot peppers or garlic.

Rabbits

Appearance: Small mammals with fur, long ears, and a penchant for eating plants.

Organic Control:

- Use physical barriers like fencing or chicken wire.
- Plant rabbit-resistant plants like daffodils, marigolds, or lavender.

Gophers and Moles

Appearance: Subterranean mammals with burrowing habits.

Organic Control:

- Use gopher baskets or wire mesh to protect plant roots.
- Install vibrating stakes or solar-powered mole-repellent devices.

Remember that maintaining a healthy garden with proper sanitation practices, crop rotation, and companion planting can help prevent pest infestations in the first place. Regularly inspect your plants for early signs of pest damage to address issues promptly and minimize damage organically.

Companion Planting

Companion planting is a gardening technique where specific plants are grown together to maximize the benefits they provide to each other. This practice is based on the idea that certain plants have natural characteristics that can help or protect neighboring plants. Companion planting can serve various purposes, including pest control, improved pollination, and enhanced soil health.

In terms of pest control, companion planting works in several ways:

Deterrence

Some plants emit natural compounds, such as strong scents or oils, that deter pests. By planting these pest-repelling plants alongside more vulnerable crops, you create a natural barrier that makes it less likely for pests to infest the area. For example, marigolds emit a strong scent that deters aphids and nematodes, making them excellent companions for other garden plants.

Attracting Beneficial Insects

Certain companion plants attract beneficial insects that feed on garden pests. For instance, plants like dill and fennel attract ladybugs and lacewings, which are natural predators of aphids and other soft-bodied insects. By planting these attractant plants near your main crops, you encourage the presence of these helpful insects.

Trap Crops

Some companion plants act as trap crops, luring pests away from valuable crops. Nasturtiums, for example, can attract aphids, drawing them away from your vegetables or ornamental plants. This can help protect your main crops from infestations.

Camouflage

Companion planting can also work by camouflaging desirable plants. By interplanting aromatic herbs or flowers among your vegetables, you can make it more challenging for pests to locate their preferred hosts. The visual and olfactory confusion can deter pests from finding and attacking specific crops.

Enhanced Diversity

A diverse garden with various plant species can disrupt pest cycles. Monoculture (planting a single crop) can create ideal conditions for pests to thrive, as they can easily move from plant to plant. Companion planting introduces diversity, making it harder for pests to establish and spread throughout the garden.

Here are a few common examples of companion planting for pest control:

Marigolds

Marigolds are known to deter various garden pests, including aphids, nematodes, and whiteflies, due to their strong scent and root secretions.

Plant marigolds around the perimeter of your garden or among susceptible crops to create a protective barrier.

Basil

Basil emits aromatic compounds that can deter flies and mosquitoes from the garden. It's particularly effective when planted near outdoor seating areas.

Basil's aroma can also help protect nearby crops, such as tomatoes, from pests like aphids and hornworms.

Lavender

Lavender attracts beneficial pollinators like bees and butterflies while repelling common garden pests like mosquitoes, moths, and fleas.

Harvest lavender flowers and use them to make natural insect repellents or sachets for wardrobes.

Chives

Chives can deter aphids, mites, and other pests due to their strong onion-like scent.

Plant chives near carrots to help improve their flavor and deter carrot flies.

Garlic

Garlic is effective in repelling a variety of pests, including aphids, beetles, and caterpillars.

Plant garlic near roses to deter aphids or around fruit trees to help prevent borers.

Dill

Dill attracts beneficial insects like ladybugs and parasitic wasps, which prey on aphids and other garden pests.

Plant dill near tomatoes, cucumbers, or squash to support these crops.

Nasturtiums

Nasturtiums not only trap aphids but also attract aphid predators like ladybugs and lacewings.

Interplant nasturtiums with brassicas (cabbage, broccoli) to help protect them from cabbage worms.

Rosemary

Rosemary has a strong aroma that can deter pests like cabbage moths, carrot flies, and bean beetles.

Plant rosemary near beans, cabbage, or carrots to help protect them.

Oregano

Oregano can repel aphids and spider mites, making it a useful companion for various garden vegetables.

Plant oregano near peppers, tomatoes, or beans to keep these crops pest-free.

Sage

Sage can deter cabbage moths and carrot flies while attracting pollinators like bees.

Plant sage near cabbage family crops and carrots for added protection.

Mint

Mint's strong scent can repel aphids, ants, and cabbage moths.

Plant mint in containers near vegetables like tomatoes and cabbages to help keep pests away.

Tansy

Tansy can deter ants, aphids, and cucumber beetles with its strong aroma.

Plant tansy near cucumbers, roses, or squash to discourage these pests.

Catnip

Catnip (Nepeta cataria) can deter flea beetles, aphids, and squash bugs.

Plant catnip near eggplants, squash, or collard greens to protect them from these pests.

These companion planting combinations not only help deter pests but also contribute to a diverse and balanced garden ecosystem. They promote natural pest control while enhancing the health and productivity of your garden.

It's important to research and plan your companion planting arrangements based on the specific pests you're dealing with and the companion plants that are most effective for your region and climate. Additionally, not all plants make good companions, so it's essential to consider compatibility and space requirements when planning your garden.

Common Plant Diseases

Just like people, plants can also get sick. This is usually because there is an imbalance somewhere. Either a lack of nutrients, a poor watering schedule, watering at the wrong time, or even pests can all contribute. These diseases can make plants look unhealthy, cause spots or changes in their leaves, or even kill them. They can be caused by tiny things like bacteria, fungi, or viruses.

The solution is, of course, to keep your plants healthy and avoid plant diseases altogether. Here are four techniques you can make use of to avoid plant diseases:

1. Crop rotation
    o   Plan a garden layout that rotates crops from year to year.

    o   This practice disrupts the life cycles of soil-borne pathogens.

    o   Avoid planting crops from the same family in the same location for consecutive years to prevent the buildup of diseases.

2. Disease-resistant varieties
    o   Research and select plant varieties known to be resistant to common diseases in your region.

- Consult with local nurseries or gardening experts for recommendations.

- Disease-resistant plants are often labeled with specific resistance traits, making them easier to identify.

3. Garden hygiene
   - Practice strict hygiene by promptly removing and disposing of any plant material showing signs of disease, including leaves, stems, and affected fruits.

   - Disinfect pruning tools between uses to prevent the transmission of diseases from one plant to another.

4. Organic mulch
   - Apply a layer of organic mulch, such as straw, wood chips, or compost, around the base of plants.

   - This not only conserves soil moisture and suppresses weeds but also acts as a barrier against soil-borne diseases.

   - Ensure that mulch is kept away from direct contact with plant stems to prevent moisture-related issues.

Often, we can follow every piece of advice and make use of all the different techniques and still end up with some sort of plant disease in our garden. Below, you will find a list of the common plant diseases you might encounter, how to identify them, and how to control them organically.

Powdery Mildew

Appearance: White, powdery spots or patches on leaves, stems, and flowers.

Organic Control:

- Spray affected plants with a mixture of water and baking soda.
- Neem oil or sulfur-based fungicides can also help prevent powdery mildew.

Downy Mildew

Appearance: Yellow or pale green spots on the upper leaf surface, with fuzzy gray or purple growth on the underside.

Organic Control:

- Improve air circulation around plants.
- Spray with a mixture of water and milk (1:1 ratio) or copper-based fungicides.

Leaf Spot

Appearance: Circular or irregular dark spots with a defined border on leaves.

Organic Control:

- Remove affected leaves.
- Apply copper-based fungicides or neem oil.

Early Blight (Tomato)

Appearance: Dark, concentric rings with a target-like appearance on tomato leaves, which may lead to yellowing and browning.

Organic Control:

- Remove infected leaves.
- Apply copper-based fungicides or use a baking soda spray.

Late Blight (Tomato and Potato)

Appearance: Water-soaked, dark lesions on leaves, stems, and fruit, often with a white, fuzzy growth in humid conditions.

Organic Control:

- Remove infected leaves and destroy them.
- Use copper-based fungicides or spray with a mixture of milk and water (1:1 ratio).

Botrytis (Gray Mold)

Appearance: Gray, fuzzy mold covering flowers, leaves, and fruit.

Organic Control:

- Cut off affected areas.
- Improve air circulation.
- Apply sulfur-based fungicides or neem oil.

Rust

Appearance: Yellow, orange, or rust-colored pustules or spots on leaves, stems, and fruit.

Organic Control:

- Remove infected leaves.
- Improve plant spacing.
- Apply sulfur-based fungicides.

Apple Scab

Appearance: Dark, scaly lesions on leaves and fruit that resemble scabs.

Organic Control:

- Remove infected leaves and fruit.
- Apply copper-based fungicides or neem oil.

Fire Blight (Apple and Pear)

Appearance: Wilting, blackened, or scorched-looking leaves, resembling fire damage.

Organic Control:

- Prune infected branches 8-12 inches below affected areas.
- Sterilize pruning tools between cuts.
- Apply copper-based fungicides.

Cucumber Mosaic Virus

Appearance: Distorted or mottled leaves with mosaic-like patterns and stunted growth.

Organic Control:

- Remove infected plants.
- Control aphids, which spread the virus.
- Use row covers to protect cucurbits.

Tomato Mosaic Virus

Appearance: Mottled, distorted leaves with yellow or green mosaic patterns.

Organic Control:

- Remove infected plants.
- Control aphids and other sap-sucking insects.
- Use resistant tomato varieties.

Fusarium Wilt

Appearance: Yellowing, wilting, and eventual collapse of the plant, often affecting one side first.

Organic Control:

- Plant resistant varieties.
- Improve soil drainage.
- Rotate crops.
- Avoid overwatering.

Verticillium Wilt

Appearance: Yellowing, wilting, and browning of leaves, often on one side of the plant.

Organic Control:

- Plant resistant varieties.
- Improve soil health through organic matter and proper watering.

Root Rot

Appearance: Wilting, yellowing, and stunted growth. Roots may appear brown, mushy, or discolored.

Organic Control:

- Improve soil drainage.
- Avoid overwatering.
- Apply beneficial nematodes to control root rot pathogens.

Apple Canker

Appearance: Sunken, dark lesions, or cankers on branches or the main trunk.

Organic Control:

- Prune infected branches during the dormant season.
- Remove affected bark and sterilize tools between cuts.

Peach Leaf Curl

Appearance: Curling, red, or purple leaves that may blister or have a powdery appearance.

Organic Control:

- Apply a copper-based fungicide during the dormant season.
- Improve air circulation.

Sooty Mold

Appearance: Black, soot-like growth on leaves, stems, and fruit, often associated with honeydew-producing insects.

Organic Control:

- Control the honeydew-producing insects (aphids, mealybugs).
- Use neem oil or soap and water spray to deter these insects.

Bean Rust

Appearance: Reddish-brown or orange rust-like pustules on leaves, often leading to leaf yellowing and defoliation.

Organic Control:

- Plant resistant varieties.
- Space plants for better air circulation.
- Apply sulfur-based fungicides.

Onion Downy Mildew

Appearance: Yellow-green to white, angular lesions on onion leaves, accompanied by white, fluffy growth on the underside.

Organic Control:

- Rotate crops.
- Improve soil drainage.
- Plant onions in well-drained soil.

Citrus Canker

Appearance: Raised, corky lesions or cankers on leaves, fruit, and stems.

Organic Control:

- Remove infected leaves and fruit.
- Apply copper-based fungicides.

Recognizing these symptoms and using organic control methods can help you manage and prevent these common plant diseases in your gardens effectively.

When it comes to successful pest and disease management, it is all about regular monitoring. Implement a routine for inspecting your garden for signs of pests or diseases. Early detection allows for swift intervention. Monitor the undersides of leaves, where pests often hide, and look for symptoms like wilting, discoloration, or unusual growth patterns.

By meticulously incorporating these strategies and practices, you can establish a garden that not only thrives but also serves as a balanced ecosystem where beneficial organisms help keep pests and diseases in check, ultimately reducing the need for chemical interventions.

Tip: Another great strategy in pest management is to install bird feeders or bird baths to attract insectivorous birds like sparrows, chickadees, and wrens. Also consider planting bird-attracting flowers, such as sunflowers, coneflowers, or native wildflowers, to provide additional food sources for birds.

CHAPTER 8:

Cultivating a Vegetable Garden

B y now, I know you are just burning with desire to get started on your garden; luckily this chapter brings you one step closer to planting all the edibles you desire. First, let's talk about when to plant.

The timing for planting vegetables depends on your local climate and growing zone. You can find recommended planting dates for your area by consulting local gardening resources, cooperative extension offices, or gardening apps. An excellent site to get information on when to plant different types of plants is the USDA Hardiness Zones.

Gardening zones, often represented by USDA Hardiness Zones, indicate the average minimum winter temperatures in your region. Knowing your zone helps you select plants that can thrive in your area. You can find your zone on the USDA website or in gardening books and websites specific to your country or region.

Now, let's look at 30 of the easiest and most popular edibles for you to start out with. In the section to follow, we will look at

- what to grow.
- when to plant.
- some companion plants.
- how and when to harvest.
- how to store your freshly harvested greens.

30 Easy-to-Grow Edibles

These planting guidelines will help you get started with a successful vegetable garden.

Tomatoes

When to Plant

Start seeds indoors 6-8 weeks before the last frost date in your area, then transplant after the last frost.

Companion Plant

Basil - planting basil nearby can improve tomato flavor and deter certain pests.

How to Plant

Choose a sunny spot, provide support for the plants, and space them 2-3 feet apart.

Green Beans

When to Plant

Plant green bean seeds directly in the garden after the last frost date.

Companion Plant

Plant with corn and summer savory to deter pests.

How to Plant

Sow seeds 1 inch deep, 2-4 inches apart, in rows.

Zucchini

When to Plant

Plant zucchini seeds or transplants after the last frost date in warm soil.

Companion Plant

Nasturtiums can deter squash bugs when planted nearby.

How to Plant

Space zucchini plants 3-4 feet apart in well-drained soil.

Lettuce

When to Plant

Plant lettuce seeds in early spring or late summer for a fall crop.

Companion Plant

Plant lettuce near carrots and radishes to maximize space.

How to Plant

Sow seeds shallowly and keep the soil consistently moist.

Carrots

When to Plant

Plant carrot seeds in early spring or late summer.

Companion Plant

Plant with chives, which may deter carrot flies.

How to Plant

Sow seeds directly into loose, sandy soil.

Radishes

When to Plant

Plant radish seeds as soon as the soil can be worked in early spring.

Companion Plant

Plant radishes with cucumbers to repel cucumber beetles.

How to Plant

Sow seeds directly and thin as they grow.

Cucumbers

When to Plant

Plant cucumber seeds after the last frost date when the soil is warm.

Companion Plant

Plant with marigolds or nasturtiums to deter pests.

How to Plant

Provide vertical support or trellising for vining varieties.

Peppers (Bell and Chili)

When to Plant

Start pepper seeds indoors 8–10 weeks before the last frost date, then transplant.

Companion Plant

Plant basil near peppers to improve flavor.

How to Plant

Space pepper plants 18–24 inches apart in well-drained soil.

Spinach

When to Plant

Plant spinach seeds early in spring or late in summer for a fall crop.

Companion Plant

Plant with lettuce and radishes for efficient space usage.

How to Plant

Sow seeds and keep the soil consistently moist.

Kale

When to Plant

Kale is a cool-season crop, so plant seeds in early spring or late summer.

Companion Plant

Plant with beets to deter aphids.

How to Plant

Space kale plants 12–18 inches apart in fertile soil.

Peas

When to Plant

Plant pea seeds directly in the garden as soon as the soil can be worked in early spring.

Companion Plant

Plant peas near carrots to improve soil nitrogen.

How to Plant

Provide trellises or support for climbing varieties.

Basil

When to Plant

Start basil seeds indoors 6-8 weeks before the last frost date, then transplant.

Companion Plant

Plant basil near tomatoes for improved flavor.

How to Plant

Space basil plants 12-18 inches apart in well-drained soil.

Mint

When to Plant

Plant mint from cuttings or purchased plants in spring or early summer.

Companion Plant

Mint can deter aphids, so plant it near susceptible crops.

How to Plant

Grow mint in containers or in an area with boundaries, as it can become invasive.

Chives

When to Plant

Plant chive seeds or transplants in early spring.

Companion Plant

Chives can deter aphids and improve the flavor of carrots and tomatoes.

How to Plant

Space chive plants 6-12 inches apart in well-drained soil.

Cilantro

When to Plant

Sow cilantro seeds directly in the garden in early spring or late summer.

Companion Plant

Plant cilantro near tomatoes to improve their flavor.

How to Plant

Sow seeds shallowly and thin as they grow.

Parsley

When to Plant

Plant parsley seeds or transplants in early spring.

Companion Plant

Parsley can improve the flavor of tomatoes and asparagus.

How to Plant

Space parsley plants 6-12 inches apart in well-drained soil.

Thyme

When to Plant

Plant thyme from cuttings or purchased plants in spring.

Companion Plant

Thyme is a beneficial herb for various crops and pollinators.

How to Plant

Grow thyme in well-drained soil with full sun.

Rosemary

When to Plant

Plant rosemary from cuttings or purchased plants in spring.

Companion Plant

Rosemary can deter cabbage moths and bean beetles.

How to Plant

Grow rosemary in well-drained soil with full sun.

Oregano

When to Plant

Plant oregano from cuttings or purchased plants in spring.

Companion Plant

Oregano can improve the flavor of beans and broccoli.

How to Plant

Grow oregano in well-drained soil with full sun.

Dill

When to Plant

Sow dill seeds directly in the garden after the last frost date.

Companion Plant
Plant dill near tomatoes and cucumbers to improve their flavor.

How to Plant
Space dill plants 12-18 inches apart in well-drained soil.

Onions (Green and Bulb)
When to Plant
Plant onion sets for green onions early in spring. Plant bulb onions from sets in early spring.

Companion Plant
Onions can deter aphids and carrot flies. Plant with carrots to improve soil health.

How to Plant
Space onion sets 1-2 inches apart for green onions, and 4-6 inches apart for bulb onions.

Beets
When to Plant
Plant beet seeds directly in the garden as soon as the soil can be worked in early spring.

Companion Plant
Beets grow well with bush beans and lettuce.

How to Plant
Sow beet seeds 1 inch apart and thin them as they grow.

Squash (Summer and Winter)

When to Plant

Plant squash seeds or transplants after the last frost date in warm soil.

Companion Plant

Nasturtiums can deter squash bugs when planted nearby.

How to Plant

Space squash plants 3-4 feet apart for summer squash and 4-6 feet apart for winter squash.

Eggplants

When to Plant

Start eggplant seeds indoors 8-10 weeks before the last frost date, then transplant.

Companion Plant

Plant basil or marigolds near eggplants to deter pests.

How to Plant

Space eggplant plants 18-24 inches apart in well-drained soil.

Potatoes

When to Plant

Plant seed potatoes in early spring in mounds or containers.

Companion Plant

Plant potatoes with beans and corn for a "three sisters" garden.

How to Plant

Space seed potatoes 12 inches apart in rows or mounds.

Swiss Chard

When to Plant

Plant Swiss chard seeds early in spring or late in summer.

Companion Plant

Swiss chard can grow well with onions and garlic.

How to Plant

Space Swiss chard plants 6-8 inches apart in well-drained soil.

Arugula

When to Plant

Sow arugula seeds directly in the garden in early spring or late summer.

Companion Plant

Plant arugula near basil and lettuce for a salad garden.

How to Plant

Sow arugula seeds shallowly and keep the soil consistently moist.

Mustard Greens

When to Plant

Plant mustard green seeds directly in the garden in early spring or late summer.

Companion Plant

Mustard greens grow well with beets and mint.

How to Plant

Sow seeds shallowly and thin them as they grow.

Celery

When to Plant

Plant celery from the base of store-bought celery in spring or early summer.

Companion Plant

Celery can be grown with beans and tomatoes.

How to Plant

Space celery plants 6-12 inches apart in well-drained soil.

Broccoli

When to Plant

Start broccoli seeds indoors 6-8 weeks before the last frost date, then transplant.

Companion Plant

Plant broccoli with onions or herbs like rosemary.

How to Plant

Space broccoli plants 18-24 inches apart in well-drained soil.

How to Harvest and Store

Tomatoes

When to Harvest

Harvest when the tomatoes are firm, fully colored, and have a glossy appearance.

Harvesting Practices

Gently twist or cut tomatoes from the vine to avoid damaging the plant.

Storing and Preserving

Store ripe tomatoes at room temperature away from direct sunlight. Refrigerate only if fully ripe, and to extend shelf life, make tomato sauce or can them.

Green Beans

When to Harvest

Harvest green beans when they are young and tender before the seeds inside the pods become too large.

Harvesting Practices

Use two hands to snap or cut beans from the plant to prevent damage.

Storing and Preserving

Store in the refrigerator for a few days or blanch and freeze for long-term storage.

Zucchini

When to Harvest

Harvest zucchini when they are about 6-8 inches long for the best flavor and texture.

Harvesting Practices

Use a sharp knife to cut zucchinis from the plant without damaging the vines.

Storing and Preserving

Store in the refrigerator for up to a week or grate zucchini and freeze it.

Lettuce

When to Harvest

Harvest lettuce leaves when they are young and tender before they bolt (flower and go to seed).

Harvesting Practices

Cut leaves at the base, leaving the central growth point intact for regrowth.

Storing and Preserving

Store washed and dried lettuce leaves in a plastic bag with a paper towel to absorb moisture, and refrigerate for a few days.

Carrots

When to Harvest

Harvest carrots when they reach the desired size and color.

Harvesting Practices

Gently loosen the soil around carrots and pull them out by grasping the foliage.

Storing and Preserving

Store carrots in a cool, humid place, like a root cellar, or refrigerate in a plastic bag with some moisture to prevent wilting.

Radishes

When to Harvest

Harvest radishes when they are about the size of a large marble.

Harvesting Practices

Gently pull radishes out of the soil, removing the tops.

Storing and Preserving

Remove radish greens and store the roots in the refrigerator.

Cucumbers

When to Harvest

Harvest cucumbers when they are dark green, firm, and about 6-8 inches long.

Harvesting Practices

Use scissors or a knife to cut cucumbers from the vine to avoid damaging the plant.

Storing and Preserving

Store in the refrigerator and use within a week for the best flavor.

Peppers (Bell and Chili)

When to Harvest

Harvest peppers when they reach their mature color and size.

Harvesting Practices

Use scissors or a sharp knife to cut peppers from the plant.

Storing and Preserving

Store peppers in the refrigerator or freeze them for long-term use.

Spinach

When to Harvest

Harvest spinach when the leaves are young and tender before they bolt.

Harvesting Practices

Cut individual leaves or use the "cut and come again" method by trimming the outer leaves, allowing the center to grow.

Storing and Preserving

Store in the refrigerator for a few days.

Kale

When to Harvest

Harvest kale leaves when they are young and tender for the best flavor.

Harvesting Practices

Remove the outer leaves or use the "cut and come again" method.

Storing and Preserving

Store in the refrigerator for up to a week.

Peas

When to Harvest

Harvest peas when the pods are plump and the peas inside are full-sized but not overly mature.

Harvesting Practices

Gently pick peas from the vines to avoid damaging them.

Storing and Preserving
Shell and freeze peas for long-term storage.

Basil
When to Harvest
Harvest basil leaves once the plant has several sets of leaves and before it flowers for the best flavor.

Harvesting Practices
Pinch off individual leaves or prune the plant by cutting just above a set of leaves.

Storing and Preserving
Store basil leaves in the refrigerator or make pesto and freeze it for longer storage.

Mint
When to Harvest
Harvest mint leaves as needed throughout the growing season.

Harvesting Practices
Pinch or snip off leaves as required.

Storing and Preserving
Store fresh mint leaves in a plastic bag in the refrigerator. You can also dry mint leaves for later use.

Chives
When to Harvest
Harvest chive leaves once they reach a sufficient length.

Harvesting Practices

Cut chives about an inch above the ground to encourage regrowth.

Storing and Preserving

Store fresh chives in the refrigerator or chop and freeze them.

Cilantro

When to Harvest

Harvest cilantro leaves before the plant bolts and the leaves become bitter.

Harvesting Practices

Cut or snip off individual leaves.

Storing and Preserving

Store cilantro in the refrigerator with the stems in water or freeze chopped cilantro.

Parsley

When to Harvest

Harvest parsley leaves as needed throughout the growing season.

Harvesting Practices

Cut leaves from the outer portion of the plant.

Storing and Preserving

Store parsley in the refrigerator or freeze it for later use.

Thyme

When to Harvest

Harvest thyme leaves once the plant has grown sufficiently.

Harvesting Practices

Snip or pinch off thyme leaves as needed.

Storing and Preserving

Dry thyme leaves and store them in an airtight container.

Rosemary

When to Harvest

Harvest rosemary sprigs once the plant is established.

Harvesting Practices

Snip rosemary sprigs as needed.

Storing and Preserving

Fresh rosemary can be stored in the refrigerator. You can also dry rosemary for long-term use.

Oregano

When to Harvest

Harvest oregano leaves throughout the growing season.

Harvesting Practices

Snip off oregano leaves.

Storing and Preserving

Dry oregano leaves and store them in an airtight container.

Dill

When to Harvest

Harvest dill leaves just before the plant flowers.

Harvesting Practices

Cut or snip dill leaves or the entire umbel (flower cluster).

Storing and Preserving

Store fresh dill in the refrigerator or freeze it.

Onions (Green and Bulb)

When to Harvest

Harvest green onions when they reach the desired size and bulb onions when the tops have dried and fallen over.

Harvesting Practices

Gently pull green onions or lift bulb onions from the soil.

Storing and Preserving

Cure bulb onions before storing them in a cool, dry place. Use green onions promptly.

Beets

When to Harvest

Harvest beets when they reach the desired size, typically about 1-2 inches in diameter.

Harvesting Practices

Gently pull beets from the soil and trim the greens.

Storing and Preserving

Store beets in the refrigerator, and you can also pickle or can them.

Squash (Summer and Winter)

When to Harvest

Harvest summer squash when they are young and tender, and winter squash when the skin has hardened.

Harvesting Practices

Cut squash from the plant using a sharp knife or shears.

Storing and Preserving

Store winter squash in a cool, dry place. Use summer squash within a few days.

Eggplants

When to Harvest

Harvest eggplants when they are glossy, firm, and fully colored.

Harvesting Practices

Use scissors or a knife to cut eggplants from the plant.

Storing and Preserving

Store eggplants in the refrigerator for up to a week.

Potatoes

When to Harvest

Harvest potatoes when the plants have flowered and the tops have died back.

Harvesting Practices

Gently dig up potatoes to avoid damaging them.

Storing and Preserving
Cure potatoes before storing them in a cool, dark place.

Swiss Chard
When to Harvest
Harvest Swiss chard leaves when they are young and tender.

Harvesting Practices
Cut individual leaves, leaving the central growth point for regrowth.

Storing and Preserving
Store Swiss chard leaves in the refrigerator for up to a week.

Arugula
When to Harvest
Harvest arugula leaves when they are young for the best flavor.

Harvesting Practices
Cut or snip off individual leaves or use the "cut and come again" method.

Storing and Preserving
Store arugula leaves in the refrigerator for a few days.

Mustard Greens
When to Harvest
Harvest mustard greens when the leaves are young and tender.

Harvesting Practices
Cut or snip off individual leaves or use the "cut and come again" method.

Storing and Preserving
Store mustard greens in the refrigerator for a few days.

Celery
When to Harvest
Harvest celery stalks when they have reached the desired size.

Harvesting Practices
Cut or snap off individual stalks.

Storing and Preserving
Store celery in the refrigerator. You can also blanch and freeze it for later use.

Broccoli
When to Harvest
Harvest broccoli heads when they are tight and compact.

Harvesting Practices
Cut broccoli heads at a slant to encourage side shoots.

Storing and Preserving
Store broccoli in the refrigerator and use within a few days.

By selecting easy-to-grow vegetables, planting at the right time, and considering companion planting and your gardening zone, you can set yourself up for a successful and enjoyable gardening experience as a beginner.

CHAPTER 9:

Sustainable Gardening Practices

E very healthy, thriving garden needs to be run using sustainable gardening practices. These are practices such as composting, crop rotation, and building a mini echo system that attracts beneficial insects and other wildlife.

The main objective is to create a good natural balance within your garden that is not only beneficial to the environment but also makes your work easier and delivers healthy produce for you and your family.

Composting and Recycling in the Garden

Composting is an eco-friendly practice that not only reduces waste but also enriches your garden's soil.

Here's how to start a compost pile and why it's beneficial for your garden:

Starting a Compost Pile

1. Choose a location.

   ○ Pick a well-drained spot in your garden that gets partial sunlight.

   ○ Sunlight aids in decomposition.

2. Build or purchase a bin.

   ○ Consider using a compost bin to contain materials and manage the process efficiently.

   ○ Bins also deter pests.

3. Gather ingredients.

   ○ Compost requires a balance of green (nitrogen-rich) and brown (carbon-rich) materials.

   ○ Greens include kitchen scraps (e.g., fruit peels, coffee grounds) and fresh yard waste (e.g., grass clippings).

   ○ Browns consist of dried leaves, straw, and small branches.

4. Layer materials.

   ○ Begin with a layer of brown materials at the bottom, followed by a layer of green materials.

   ○ Continue alternating between greens and browns.

- ○ Break down or shred larger items for faster decomposition.

5. Maintain moisture.

   - ○ Keep the compost pile as damp as a wrung-out sponge.

   - ○ Water it when it feels dry to the touch.

   - ○ Proper moisture levels facilitate microbial activity.

6. Aerate the pile.

   - ○ Turn the compost pile approximately once a month using a pitchfork or shovel.

   - ○ This introduces oxygen, crucial for decomposition, and ensures even breakdown.

7. Monitor temperature.

   - ○ A properly managed compost pile will naturally heat up during decomposition.

   - ○ This heat helps eliminate weed seeds and pathogens.

   - ○ Aim for a temperature range of 130–160°F (54–71°C).

8. Compost.

   - ○ Compost matures over time, typically in 6–12 months.

o   It's ready when it appears dark, crumbly, and smells earthy, without any strong odors.

Benefits of Composting and Recycling in the Garden

Enriched Soil

Compost adds essential nutrients to your garden soil, improving its fertility, structure, aeration, and water retention.

Reduced Waste

Composting reduces the amount of kitchen and yard waste sent to landfills, contributing to waste reduction and environmental sustainability.

Healthy Plants

Plants grown in compost-amended soil tend to be healthier, more vigorous, and more resistant to pests and diseases.

Cost Savings

Composting reduces the need for store-bought fertilizers and soil conditioners, saving you money in the long run.

Environmental Benefits

By recycling organic waste through composting, you help reduce greenhouse gas emissions that are typically produced in landfills.

Crop Rotation

We briefly touched on crop rotation in Chapter 7 as an effective pest management technique. However, crop rotation is much more as it helps maintain healthy soil and, in the end, helps ensure you have a healthy thriving garden.

How It works

Plan a Rotation

Divide your garden into sections or beds and move plant families to different beds each year. For instance, if you grew tomatoes in one bed this year, plant them in a different bed next year.

Diversify Plant Families

Rotate crops within the same plant family each season. Avoid planting the same family in the same bed consecutively.

1. Solanaceae (Nightshade Family)

    A. Vegetables: Tomatoes, peppers, eggplants, potatoes.

    B. Herbs: Belladonna, mandrake.

2. Brassicaceae (Cruciferous Family)

    A. Vegetables: Broccoli, cauliflower, cabbage, Brussels sprouts, kale, radishes.

    B. Herbs: None in this family, but it includes many edible crops.

3. Fabaceae (Legume Family)

    A. Vegetables: Peas, beans, lentils.

    B. Herbs: None commonly grown as herbs, but some members like clover are used for forage.

4. Apiaceae (Carrot Family)

    A. Vegetables: Carrots, celery, parsley, parsnips.

    B. Herbs: Dill, cilantro, fennel, anise, coriander.

5. Lamiaceae (Mint Family)

    A. Vegetables: None commonly grown as vegetables.

    B. Herbs: Mint, basil, rosemary, oregano, thyme, sage.

6. Asteraceae (Aster Family)

    A. Vegetables: Artichokes, lettuce, chicory, endive.

    B. Herbs: Chamomile, tarragon.

7. Cucurbitaceae (Gourd Family)

    A. Vegetables: Cucumbers, pumpkins, squashes (zucchini, butternut).

    B. Herbs: None commonly grown as herbs.

8. Alliaceae (Onion Family)

    A. Vegetables: Onions, garlic, leeks, shallots.

    B. Herbs: Chives.

9. Amaranthaceae (Amaranth Family)

    A. Vegetables: Spinach, Swiss chard, beets.

    B. Herbs: None commonly grown as herbs.

10. Poaceae (Grass Family)

    A. Vegetables: Corn (maize).

    B. Herbs: None commonly grown as herbs.

These are just a few examples of plant families, and there are many more in the plant kingdom. Understanding plant families can be helpful in crop rotation practices and identifying common characteristics and growing requirements among related plants. It can also be useful in managing pests and diseases since certain pests and diseases may affect plants within the same family.

Break Pest Cycles

Crop rotation disrupts the life cycles of pests and diseases that target specific plant families, reducing the need for chemical interventions.

Improve Soil Health

Different crops have varying nutrient requirements and effects on soil. Rotation helps balance nutrient levels and prevent soil depletion.

Benefit From Soil Microbes

Certain crops attract beneficial soil microbes. Rotating crops encourages a diverse microbial community, contributing to soil health.

Weed Control

Crop rotation can help manage weeds by disrupting weed life cycles and reducing weed pressure.

Incorporating composting, recycling, and crop rotation into your gardening practices leads to healthier plants, improved soil quality, and a more sustainable and bountiful garden.

Here's a simple example of how to rotate crops in a small garden bed over a three-year period:

Year 1: Bed A - Legumes (Peas and Beans)

1. In the first year, plant legumes like peas and beans in Bed A. These plants help fix nitrogen in the soil, enriching it for future crops.

2. After harvesting the legumes, leave the roots in the soil to decompose and continue to add nitrogen.

Year 2: Bed A - Leafy Greens (Lettuce and Spinach)

1. In the second year, plant leafy greens like lettuce and spinach in Bed A. These crops don't require as much nitrogen as others.

2. The nitrogen left in the soil from the previous year's legumes will benefit the leafy greens.

Year 3: Bed A - Root Vegetables (Carrots and Radishes)

1. In the third year, plant root vegetables like carrots and radishes in Bed A. These crops benefit from well-balanced soil with enough nitrogen.

2. The soil is now balanced and ready for root vegetables.

Year 1: Bed B - Leafy Greens (Lettuce and Spinach)

1. In the first year, while Bed A is planted with legumes, plant leafy greens like lettuce and spinach in Bed B.

2. These leafy greens help break the pest and disease cycle, as they are less susceptible to soil-borne pathogens that may have affected Bed B the previous year.

Year 2: Bed B - Root Vegetables (Carrots and Radishes)

1. In the second year, plant root vegetables like carrots and radishes in Bed B.

2. Root vegetables are less prone to the pests and diseases that affect leafy greens.

Year 3: Bed B - Legumes (Peas and Beans)

1. In the third year, plant legumes like peas and beans in Bed B.

2. These legumes will replenish the nitrogen in the soil, preparing it for future crops.

By following this three-year crop rotation plan, you can help maintain soil fertility, reduce the risk of soil-borne diseases, and deter pests that are specific to certain plant families. Additionally, this rotation plan optimizes the use of garden space and resources while improving overall garden health.

Attracting Beneficial Insects and Wildlife to Your Garden

Encouraging beneficial insects and wildlife in your garden is a smart approach to improve pest control and foster a balanced ecosystem.

Plants and Flowers for Beneficial Insects

Pollinator-Friendly Plants

Include a variety of nectar-rich flowers such as lavender, coneflowers, sunflowers, and bee balm. These plants attract pollinators like bees, butterflies, and hummingbirds, which aid in fertilizing flowers.

Herbs

Herbs like dill, fennel, and parsley attract both pollinators and beneficial insects like ladybugs, which help control pests in your garden.

Native Plants

Native plants are adapted to your region's conditions and provide valuable resources for local beneficial insects. Conduct research to determine which native plants thrive in your area and include them in your garden.

Companion Plants

Grow companion plants like marigolds, nasturtiums, and chrysanthemums. These not only deter common garden pests but also attract beneficial insects that can help keep your garden in balance.

Attracting Good Wildlife

Provide Water Sources

Install bird baths, small ponds, or shallow dishes of water to offer hydration to birds, frogs, and beneficial insects that require water for their survival.

Habitat Diversity

Foster diverse habitats within your garden by incorporating trees, shrubs, and ground cover. Deadwood, rocks, and logs provide shelter and breeding sites for various wildlife species.

Native Trees and Shrubs

Plant native trees and shrubs that offer food and shelter to birds and insects. Examples include oak trees, dogwood, and serviceberry, which can attract a range of wildlife.

Avoid Chemicals

Minimize or eliminate the use of chemical pesticides, herbicides, and fertilizers, as these can harm beneficial insects and wildlife. Embrace natural alternatives for pest control.

Bird Feeders and Bird-Attracting Plants

Bird Feeders

Install bird feeders with diverse seed options to attract a variety of bird species to your garden. Sunflower seeds, thistle, and suet are popular choices.

Native Berries

Incorporate berry-bearing shrubs like elderberry, serviceberry, and viburnum into your garden to provide a natural food source for birds.

Nectar Plants

Grow nectar-producing plants like trumpet vine, salvia, and red hot poker to attract hummingbirds, which are excellent pollinators.

Birdhouses and Nesting Sites

Place birdhouses or nesting boxes to accommodate cavity-nesting birds like bluebirds and chickadees, providing them with safe spaces to raise their young.

Beneficial Insects for Pest Control

Ladybugs

Purchase ladybugs and release them in your garden to control aphids, scale insects, and other soft-bodied pests. Ladybugs are voracious predators and can significantly reduce pest populations.

Praying Mantises

Praying mantises are efficient insect predators. You can purchase them for pest control; however, be cautious, as they may also consume beneficial insects.

Lacewings

Attract lacewings by planting nectar-rich flowers. Lacewing larvae are avid aphid hunters and can help manage aphid infestations in your garden.

Parasitic Wasps

Parasitic wasps are natural enemies of many garden pests. To encourage them, provide suitable habitats like hollow sticks or structures where they can lay their eggs in pest insects.

Ground Beetles

Ground beetles prey on slugs, snails, and other pests that dwell on the ground. To attract them, create ground cover and shelter for these beneficial insects.

By integrating these strategies, you can establish a garden ecosystem that not only keeps pests under control but also enhances the overall health and biodiversity of your garden. This balanced approach leads to a more sustainable and thriving garden environment.

CHAPTER 10:

Seasonal Gardening Tips

O ur gardens can keep us busy, but it is a good kind of busy. Throughout the year, there are different tasks and other things that we need to do. By incorporating these year-round gardening preparations and soil management practices, you'll be better equipped to meet the needs of your garden and enjoy a thriving, productive growing space throughout the seasons. Regular attention and care lead to healthier plants, increased yields, and a more sustainable garden.

Year-Round Gardening Preparations

The guidelines down below can help you maintain a successful and productive garden throughout the year. Remember to adapt them to your local climate and specific garden needs.

Year-round gardening preparations and soil management are essential for maintaining healthy, productive, and sustainable gardens.

Garden Journal

Keep a garden journal to record planting dates, varieties, weather conditions, and observations throughout the year. This helps you track successes, challenges, and trends in your garden.

Soil Testing

Regularly test your soil to assess its pH, nutrient levels, and overall health. You can purchase DIY soil testing kits or send samples to a local agricultural extension service for analysis.

Compost Maintenance

Maintain an active compost pile year-round to provide a steady supply of nutrient-rich compost for your garden. Turn the pile regularly to ensure proper decomposition.

Cover Crops

During fall and winter, plant cover crops like clover, rye, or vetch to protect and enrich the soil. Cover crops prevent erosion, suppress weeds, and improve soil structure.

Mulch or Weed Barrier

Apply mulch throughout the year to conserve soil moisture, regulate temperature, and suppress weeds. Regularly replenish mulch to maintain the desired thickness.

Mulch serves several purposes, including conserving soil moisture, regulating soil temperature, and reducing weed growth. Organic mulches also break down over time, contributing to soil health.

Choose mulch materials that suit your garden and local availability. Common choices include straw, wood chips, shredded leaves, and compost.

Spread a layer of mulch 2-4 inches deep around your plants, leaving a small gap around stems to prevent rot. For weed barriers, lay down fabric or cardboard before applying mulch.

Regularly inspect your mulch layer, replenishing it as needed to maintain the desired thickness. Proper mulch maintenance ensures its continued effectiveness in the garden.

Crop Rotation Planning

Plan crop rotations for the upcoming growing season. Consider the specific nutrient needs of different plant families and design rotations accordingly.

Garden Bed Preparation

Clean up garden beds during the fall by removing spent plants and debris. Add organic matter, such as compost or well-rotted manure, to enrich the soil.

Seed Ordering or Harvesting

Order seeds well in advance of the growing season. Consider trying new varieties or heirloom seeds to diversify your garden.

Seed Saving

Choose open-pollinated or heirloom plant varieties for seed saving. These plants produce offspring that are genetically similar to the parent plant.

Allow fruits or pods to fully ripen on the plant. For instance, collect tomato seeds when the fruits are overripe, and the seeds are well-formed.

Harvest seeds from dry or mature fruits and vegetables. For example, dry bean pods should be brown and brittle. Remove seeds and dry them thoroughly on a tray or paper towels. Store them in labeled, airtight containers.

Keep your saved seeds in a cool, dry, and dark place. A refrigerator or freezer can provide an ideal storage environment to maintain seed viability.

Tool Maintenance

Clean, sharpen, and maintain your gardening tools year-round. Properly stored and well-maintained tools will last longer and perform better.

Pest and Disease Monitoring

Keep an eye on your garden for signs of pests and diseases throughout the year. Early detection allows for prompt intervention and mitigation.

Irrigation System Maintenance

Inspect and maintain your garden irrigation system, whether it's a drip system, soaker hoses, or sprinklers, to ensure proper watering during the growing season.

Wildlife Habitat

Create habitats for beneficial insects and wildlife, such as birdhouses, pollinator-friendly plants, and small ponds. Encouraging biodiversity in your garden can enhance natural pest control.

Soil Amendments

Based on soil test results, add necessary soil amendments like lime or sulfur to adjust pH and replenish essential nutrients.

Greenhouse or Indoor Gardening

If you have a greenhouse or indoor growing space, consider starting seeds, growing herbs, or cultivating cold-hardy vegetables during the winter months.

Year-Round Education

Continually educate yourself about gardening practices, techniques, and new developments. Attend workshops, read books, and connect with local gardening clubs or online communities for knowledge-sharing.

Gardening Activities for Each Season

Spring

Soil Preparation

Spring is an excellent time to improve your soil. Test the soil's pH and nutrient levels, and amend it with compost, well-rotted manure, or organic matter as needed. Turn the soil to incorporate these amendments and break up compacted areas.

Planting

In early spring, when the soil can be worked and temperatures start to rise, sow cool-season crops like peas, spinach, lettuce, and radishes directly into the garden. Transplant frost-tender seedlings such as tomatoes and peppers after the last frost date in your area. Follow recommended spacing and planting depths.

Pruning

Pruning fruit trees, berry bushes, and roses is best done before buds break and new growth begins. Remove dead or diseased branches and shape the plants for better air circulation and light penetration.

Mulching

Apply a 2–4-inch layer of organic mulch, such as straw, wood chips, or shredded leaves, around your plants. Keep mulch away from plant stems to prevent rot and pests. Mulch helps retain soil moisture, regulate temperature, and suppress weeds.

Pest Control

Start monitoring your garden for early-season pests like aphids and cabbage worms. Consider using row covers or organic pest control methods as needed.

Summer

Watering

In the heat of summer, water deeply and consistently. Early morning is the best time to water as it allows plants to dry before evening, reducing the risk of fungal diseases.

Harvesting

Regularly harvest ripe vegetables and fruits to encourage more production. Use scissors or pruners to avoid damaging plants.

Weeding

Keep up with weeding to prevent competition for nutrients and space. A handheld weeder or hoe can make this task more manageable.

Mulching

Maintain mulch to conserve soil moisture and regulate soil temperature. Replenish mulch as it breaks down during the growing season.

Pest Control

Continue monitoring for pests and diseases. Consider using beneficial insects like ladybugs and praying mantises to control garden pests.

Seed Saving

To save seeds, ensure they are fully mature and dry before collecting. For instance, let beans and peas dry on the vine, and harvest tomato seeds when the fruits are fully ripe. Store seeds in a cool, dry place.

Fall

Harvesting

As temperatures cool, continue harvesting late-season crops like squash, pumpkins, carrots, and beets. Store root vegetables in a cool, dry place.

Cover Crops

Plant cover crops like clover, rye, or vetch to protect and enrich the soil during the winter months. These cover crops help prevent erosion and suppress weeds.

Clean-Up

Remove spent plants, including annuals, weeds, and diseased plant material, from your garden to reduce the risk of overwintering pests and diseases.

Mulching

Reapply mulch to protect the soil from winter weather and conserve moisture. Proper mulching can also prevent soil compaction.

Planting

Plant garlic cloves and onion sets in the fall for a spring harvest. Fall is also a great time to plant bulbs for spring-blooming flowers.

Pruning

Prune back perennials and shrubs as needed to prepare them for winter. Cut back dead or diseased growth and shape plants for the coming year.

Winter

Garden Planning

Use the winter months for planning next year's garden. Review your garden journal and decide which crops to grow, rotate, or try anew. Create a planting schedule.

Tool Maintenance

Clean and sharpen your garden tools, including pruners, shovels, and hoes. Store them in a dry, protected area to prevent rust.

Seed Ordering

Browse seed catalogs or order seeds online for the upcoming growing season. Consider trying new varieties or heirloom seeds.

Composting

Continue adding kitchen scraps and yard waste to your compost pile. Even in winter, the decomposition process continues, albeit at a slower pace.

Indoor Gardening

If you have space and adequate lighting, consider growing herbs or vegetables indoors during the winter months. Herbs like basil and mint can thrive on a sunny windowsill.

Wildlife Feeding

Provide bird feeders filled with seeds and suet to attract and support winter birds. Fresh water sources are essential for birds during cold weather.

Successful gardening is a dynamic journey that involves a deep understanding of your plants, your garden's environment, and the various tools and techniques at your disposal. From selecting the right location and preparing your soil to choosing the best plants for your climate and learning to combat pests and diseases naturally, you've gained valuable insights into the world of gardening. You've discovered the art of companion planting, crop rotation, and the benefits of composting and recycling to enhance soil health and reduce waste.

Furthermore, attracting beneficial insects and wildlife to your garden has been explored as a sustainable approach to pest control and ecosystem enrichment. You've learned the importance of year-round preparations and soil management, allowing you to stay ahead and maintain a productive and vibrant garden throughout the seasons.

As you embark on your gardening journey, remember that it's a continuous learning process. Each year brings new experiences and challenges, and your garden will evolve with time. Embrace experimentation, creativity, and the joy of nurturing life from seed to harvest. Gardening is not only about cultivating plants; it's about fostering a deeper connection to the natural world and reaping the countless rewards it offers. With patience, dedication, and a touch of green-thumb magic, your garden can flourish and become a place of beauty, sustenance, and inspiration.

CONCLUSION

Gardening is a rich and multifaceted pursuit that blends art and science while offering a profound sense of fulfillment. It is an exploration of life's cycle, from nurturing seeds into flourishing plants to witnessing nature's marvels unfold under your care. However, its beauty and significance extend far beyond the visual appeal of blooming flowers and bountiful vegetables. Gardening is a wellspring of diverse benefits that enrich your life in numerous ways.

Imagine the simple pleasure of harvesting sun-ripened tomatoes, savoring their unmatched flavor, and knowing that they grew from your labor and care. Picture the tranquility that descends upon you as you immerse yourself in the garden, reconnecting with the rhythms of the natural world and alleviating stress. Consider the sense of community that flourishes as you share the fruits of your labor with neighbors and friends, forging bonds through the common love of gardening.

But gardening is not merely a leisurely pursuit; it is a journey that imparts knowledge, nurtures environmental stewardship, and cultivates self-sufficiency. Understanding your gardening space is the pivotal first step on this journey. By meticulously assessing variables like sunlight, soil quality, and other critical factors, you create an environment where your plants can thrive. Careful planning, protection, and ongoing maintenance ensure that your garden becomes a living testament to your dedication and harmonious coexistence with the natural world.

Equipped with this knowledge and these strategies, you are well-prepared for the ever-evolving journey of gardening. We have also delved into the indispensable tools and supplies essential for your success. These recommendations cater to beginners, but they also offer valuable insights for seasoned gardeners. Moreover, we have explored the vital components of gardening, from the intricacies of soil and fertilizers to the selection of high-quality seeds from reputable suppliers.

Understanding your soil is paramount as different soil types exhibit unique characteristics that influence water retention, drainage, and nutrient availability. Starting seeds and nurturing seedlings constitute a critical phase in gardening, laying the solid foundation upon which your success will be built. Moreover, by allowing some of your crops to go to seed each season, you can collect seeds for future planting, thus reducing your dependence on purchasing seeds or seedlings.

Recognizing the specific watering needs of different plant species in your garden is another key aspect of successful gardening. We have highlighted the factors that influence these needs, including native habitat, drought tolerance, and water preferences. Furthermore, we have explored eco-friendly practices such as rainwater harvesting using rain barrels, which not only reduce your water bills but also conserve precious resources. The importance of regular maintenance and monitoring of your irrigation system has been emphasized to prevent water wastage and ensure the health of your plants.

Sustainable gardening practices are the cornerstone of a thriving and environmentally responsible garden. Composting, crop rotation, and the creation of a miniature ecosystem that attracts beneficial insects and wildlife are all fundamental techniques. These practices aim to establish a natural balance within your garden that not only benefits the environment but also streamlines your gardening efforts and yields healthier produce for you and your family.

Understanding plant families can be a valuable asset in crop rotation practices, aiding in the identification of common characteristics and growing requirements among related plants. It can also play a pivotal role in managing pests and diseases, as certain issues may affect plants within the same family. By integrating these strategies into your gardening approach, you can cultivate a garden ecosystem that not only keeps pests in check but also enhances overall health and biodiversity.

Year-round gardening preparations and soil management are critical for maintaining a garden that is healthy, productive, and sustainable. Your journey into gardening is a dynamic one, requiring a deep understanding of your plants, your garden's environment, and the various tools and techniques at your disposal.

From selecting the ideal location and preparing your soil to choosing the best-suited plants for your climate and mastering natural pest and disease control, you have gained invaluable insights into the world of gardening. You have also discovered the art of companion planting, crop rotation, and the benefits of composting and recycling in enhancing soil health and minimizing waste. Furthermore, you have explored the practice of attracting beneficial insects and wildlife to your garden as a sustainable approach to pest control and ecosystem enrichment.

As you embark on your gardening journey, remember that it is a continuous process of learning and growth. Each year brings new experiences and challenges, and your garden will evolve with time. Embrace experimentation, kindle your creativity, and take delight in nurturing life from seed to harvest. Gardening is not just about cultivating plants; it is about forging a profound connection with the natural world and reaping the countless rewards it offers.

With patience, dedication, and a touch of green-thumb magic, your garden can flourish and evolve into a sanctuary of beauty, sustenance, and inspiration. As you conclude this chapter of your gardening journey, take pride in your accomplishments. Embrace gardening as a lifelong passion, learn from your experiences, and consider expanding your garden further with the addition of flowers, trees, greenhouses, and more. Your garden is a testament to your commitment to nature and your enduring relationship with the land.

REFERENCES

Andrychowicz, A. (2018, April 5). *How to determine sun exposure in your garden*. Get Busy Gardening. https://getbusygardening.com/how-to-determine-sun-exposure/

Ask a pro gardener: Our year-round garden maintenance checklist. (2023, April 3). Lawn Troopers. https://lawntroopers.com/ask-a-pro-gardener-our-year-round-garden-maintenance-checklist/

Boeckmann, C. (2023a, May 16). *Vegetable gardening for beginners*. Old Farmer's Almanac. https://www.almanac.com/vegetable-gardening-for-beginners

Boeckmann, C. (2023b, September 5). *10 easy vegetables to grow from seed*. Old Farmer's Almanac. https://www.almanac.com/content/10-easy-vegetables-grow-seed

Godman, H. (2012, June 29). *Backyard gardening: Grow your own food, improve your health*. Harvard Health Blog.

https://www.health.harvard.edu/blog/backyard-gardening-grow-your-own-food-improve-your-health-201206294984

How to design the perfect vegetable garden layout. (2022, March 28). Plant Perfect. https://plantperfect.com/how-to-design-the-perfect-vegetable-garden-layout/#:~:text=Design%20in%20Rows

McLaughlin, C. (2009, September 29). *What is sustainable gardening?* FineGardening. https://www.finegardening.com/article/what-is-sustainable-gardening

National Agricultural Library. (n.d.). *Vegetable gardening.* U.S. Department of Agriculture. https://www.nal.usda.gov/plant-production-gardening/vegetable-gardening

Neveln, V. (2023a, February 13). *How to understand your yard's sunlight so you know what to plant where.* Better Homes & Gardens. https://www.bhg.com/gardening/how-to-garden/understanding-your-yard-s-sunlight/#:~:text=Study%20Your%20Yard

Neveln, V. (2023b, September 8). *25 gardening tips you'll wish you'd known sooner.* Better Homes & Gardens. https://www.bhg.com/gardening/yard/garden-care/gardening-tips-for-every-gardener/

Sandercock, P. (2020, April 23). *How to start a vegetable garden*. Canadian Food Focus. https://canadianfoodfocus.org/in-your-kitchen/how-to-start-a-vegetable-garden/

SanSone, A. E. (2023, March 29). *Read this before you start a vegetable garden*. Country Living. https://www.countryliving.com/gardening/garden-ideas/g43413616/vegetable-garden-for-beginners/

Sharples, A. (2020, April 21). *Your guide to different soil types*. Garden Benches Blog. https://www.gardenbenches.com/blog/different-soil-types/

Stockigt, S. (2021, January 11). *Growing a veggie garden for beginners*. Life Is a Garden. https://www.lifeisagarden.co.za/growing-a-veggie-patch-for-beginners/#:~:text=Sowing%20a%20couple%20of%20seeds

Sweetser, R. (2023, May 6). *Top 10 gardening tips for beginners*. Almanac.com. https://www.almanac.com/10-tips-beginner-gardeners

Vegetable gardening for beginners. (2022, November 28). Gardeners Supply Company. https://www.gardeners.com/how-to/vegetable-gardening/5069.html

Will, M. J. (2022, June 14). *Full sun to shade: How to assess light conditions in your garden*. Empress of Dirt. https://empressofdirt.net/light-conditions/

Made in the USA
Coppell, TX
24 January 2025

44922365R00118